HOW TO
BREAK INTO THE
MEDIA PROFESSIONS

Also by Caroline A. Zimmermann

THE SUPER SNEAKER BOOK

YOUR CHILD CAN BE A MODEL

How to Break into the Media Professions

by
Caroline A. Zimmermann

A Dolphin Book
DOUBLEDAY & COMPANY, INC.
Garden City, New York
1981

Library of Congress Cataloging in Publication Data

Zimmermann, Caroline A   1944-
  How to break into the media professions.

  Bibliography.
  1. Mass media—Vocational guidance.   I. Title.
P91.6.Z5   302.2'3
ISBN: 0-385-15934-X
Library of Congress Catalog Card Number 80-6665

DEDICATION

To Jeffrey . . . Whose love, humor and guidance have brought me more than I could possibly acknowledge.

ACKNOWLEDGMENTS

To my editor, Lindy Hess, who (once again!) has proved invaluable in her assistance and helped me to shape this book, a special thank you.

To Laura Van Wormer, my assistant editor, who brought her enormous energy and enthusiasm to this project, many thanks.

To Linda Burnham, Henry Joseph Scott, Druanne Dillon, and Risa Bell, who helped make this book a reality, I thank you.

Special acknowledgment to the following:

Heidi Bermacher	John Pahmer
Chip Block	Jim Pettijohn
RoseMarie Brooks	Parker Ransom
Cynthia Clark	Suzanne Roper
Martin Cohn	Lory Roston
Ed Cooperman	Jay Rubin
Bob DeLay	Richard Sachinis
Jeffrey Feinman	Timothy Sharpe
Benita Fury	David Shepard
Pamela Fiori	Bob Silverman
Alex Gotfryd	Peyton Sise
Bernice Grossman	Malcolm Smith
Binnie Held	Carolyn Sollis
Charlotte Kelly	Jack Stern
Peter Kerr	Richard Story
Jared Kieling	Annette Swanstrom
Steve Lawrence	Linda Taber
John Marinello	Marcia Vickery
Thomas Moore	Richard Weiner
Bo Niles	Jane Wolchonok

Contents

PART II   BREAKING INTO THE MEDIA PROFESSIONS

Introduction

"Although it's true that the media communications fields are tough to crack at the entry level, I believe there would be a lot more opportunities, and jobs landed, if these kids just knew *how* to look for them."

mass media executive

* Paul has sent out hundreds of résumés in his search for a job in publishing. Six months out of school, dozens of interviews later, and he still has nothing.

* Janet has been running classified ads stating that "she'll work at anything in television" if someone will just give her work.

* Bob's father has used his contacts to set up interviews so that Bob could find out about advertising. But no one has offered him a job.

* Katie reads the classifieds every Sunday, follows them up with a résumé, but somehow, nothing ever comes through.

* Dave interviewed for the position of researcher at a special interest magazine, but was offered a job as a clerk/typist. He turned it down.

These young people are all well-educated, bright, and in some cases, quite talented. They've all been "looking" for jobs in the media professions for months with no success. Several have been rejected a number of times while others haven't even had a nibble. They're all pretty discouraged, and frankly, they're all about to give up looking for that dream career in media and drift to other fields where they can get employment.

What is the problem? Each has more than the needed qualifications for an entry-level position. They have all written letters, used contacts, and left résumés everywhere. They've seen employment agencies and applied for any number of openings. Yet nothing has happened.

It's not surprising. The competition is fierce. Last year, for example, at one New York publishing house, there were 159 openings for jobs at the entry level. And there were nearly 10,000 applicants for those jobs!

If you want to break into one of the media professions, then you have to make sure that you're the one with that competitive edge—to prove that you're better qualified than any of the other applicants.

Now, this doesn't mean that you've got to be brighter or better educated, or more talented (although admittedly, all this helps) than the others, but it does mean that you're going to have to "get smart." This means that you've got to indoctrinate yourself with everything there is to know about your field—and this includes *how* to get a job in that field.

If you're willing to do whatever is necessary to get yourself started, if you're willing to explore all the routes that are available, if you're willing to risk rejection after rejection, then you'll probably be able to break into the media profession of your choice—despite that tough competition.

If you're interested in any of the media professions, and for the purpose of this book they are defined as book, magazine and newspaper publishing, advertising, public relations, broadcasting and film, then the first thing you've got to know is that the world of media communications is like no other. It's challenging, exciting, stimulating, rewarding, and downright fun. But it's also dull, boring, exasperating, and incredibly difficult. There are few other professions that will require the work, the dedication, and the determination that these require of you. "Above and beyond the call of duty," as one advertising executive phrased it.

With all this in mind, let's see what can be done to get you going. The purpose of this book is twofold. First, it serves to give you the basic guidance and practical hints you need to look for a job, the foundation that will help give you the competitive edge. Second, this book will get you thinking for yourself about some of the important questions involved in launching your career in one of the media professions. What you should know—what executives are looking for—to help you to stand out from the crowd.

First of all, let's examine your education. Suppose you are a graduate art historian. Does that mean you are limited in the kinds of jobs for which you can apply? No, but it does mean that you may have to take some additional courses in order to break into the media professions. Even if you have an MBA or a master's, with a major in media, and school or summer jobs as experience, you're still likely to find that they only count for a little extra in that job search. That's a fact of life. This book will help you to assess your qualifications so you'll know what course of action to take.

Remember that most media jobs are so popular, and so much in demand, that the level of education is just a starting point. The study of English, visual arts, psychology, and other liberal arts subjects are useful and will become handy in many situations throughout life. But because you are trying to start a career without commercial experience (or very little of it, at best), you must get "hands-on" training. And in order to get that training, you must learn on the job, usually at an entry-level position.

When starting, no matter how hard you have studied, you can't thoroughly know a job or an industry. It is unrealistic, especially in this highly competitive field, to expect to begin with a top job at a good salary. What employers seek in an applicant for an entry-level position are the basic skills and qualities needed for the job at hand. And precisely because there are so many applicants in media, they can demand intangible qualities (such as enthusiasm, desire, attitude) that go far beyond the basic skills.

Customarily, it is from the entry-level ranks that higher-level positions are filled. So being willing to consider an entry-level position is not a put-down (as so many young people think), *it is an opportunity in which to start on the media ladder*. What you do after beginning the job is up to you. The openings and opportunities will then be a broad invitation to utilize your initiative, abilities, education, personality, curiosity, leadership, contacts, manual skills, and other qualities.

Once you start on a job, you are in a position to utilize advantages as they appear. The more you learn and the more that people get to know you, the better your chance to advance. That, typically, is the way to move up.

There are many significant subjects covered in this book. Some help you explore your inner self while others look into the professions themselves. May you use them well, with successful results awaiting you as you move closer to breaking into the media professions and beginning your communications career.

HOW TO
BREAK INTO THE
MEDIA PROFESSIONS

Part I

Launching
Yourself

Chapter 1

IT'S NOT WHO YOU KNOW,
BUT WHAT YOU KNOW

You may assume that the term *media* includes publishing, broadcasting via television or radio, advertising, public relations, and many related forms of communication. Generally, that is the main career direction explored in this book. But there are many other areas you can consider, if you seek a career in media. Your own outlook, and ways you perceive things that influence you, can open your mind to a wealth of other media. Some can be quite exciting, satisfying, and rewarding. The possibilities are enormous, and challenging.

THE DEFINITION OF MEDIA

Start with the dictionary. *Media* is the plural of *medium*. As in Webster's Unabridged: "Medium: Something through or by which something is accomplished, conveyed, or carried on . . . an intermediate or direct instrumentality or means . . . a channel, method . . . as an advertising medium." You can go anywhere, with that kind of opening.

Media is the buzz word for entire industries and means of communications. Schools have changed "libraries" into "Media Centers," part of which contain books. But also included are magazines, newspapers, microfilm, maps, tape recordings, film strips, slides, movies, phonograph records, video tapes, special exhibits, and a wide range of other audio/visual materials.

Media, in essence, is a means by which human beings gain an understanding of the many and varying natures of their environment. In understanding the environment, people gain the capability and sometimes the desire to control it, and if necessary, change it. Through the use of radio, television, films, books, newspapers, magazines, public relations, advertising, and a wide range of other media, the world's population is influenced. The world of media is constantly changing. New opportunities are continually opening up. So, if you'd like to have a media career, don't let yourself be confined by current or rigid definitions as to what the word means. It has infinite scope, in a wealth of applications. You don't have to be in a standard "media profession" to have a media career and if you want to, you can break away from routes you normally thought were fixed and unchangeable.

LOOKING FOR A JOB IN MEDIA

You're likely to find on your job search that some executives are looking for specialists, others, liberal arts graduates, and still others, experienced people only. And then there are those who respond to the individual's personality, appearance, willingness, enthusiasm, and attitude. You never know what will result in acceptance or rejection when job hunting. But one thing is sure: new people are continually being broken into various starting-level media jobs and one of them might as well be you!

So what's involved? "I believe you have to know the name of the job you want, or at least the responsibilities of that job," says Bernice Grossman, Circulation Director for *Co-ed* magazine. "You should research the company before you apply," she continues, "and you should have a good idea of what you want to do. I find that too many young people don't even understand the basics of the field in which they are interested.

"The competition is too tough to be general when you are looking for a job. The people who are hiring know what kind of job they want filled. When I ask someone what they want to do, I want a pretty specific answer. I want them to know in advance what they want—not to be figuring it out on the job."

Knowing what you want in advance means starting at the very beginning.

In general, entry-level jobs in media inspire strong competition, since job seekers far outnumber job openings. Many aspects of these media jobs make them attractive: the glamorous image, opportunity to meet famous people, national or international exposure, high-level excitement. All of these jobs have their share of tedium as well, found in such necessary activities as filing reports, writing proposals, making contacts, checking facts, and follow-up.

Though competition may be fierce for these positions, it is reassuring to know that jobs in the media fields are continually opening up. And as long as applicants are being considered, you probably have the potential to land one of these jobs. You could crack the communications field by accepting a job that offers chances for advancement, or chances to learn about upcoming jobs, or by starting out in a small town, rather than going straight to one of the more competitive media centers, such as New York or Los Angeles. These kinds of "sacrifices" can—and often do!—make the difference between getting the jobs in media and accepting work in less appealing areas.

Add to this the value of a broad education in the subject matter about which you will be communicating. The more areas you know, the better you can perform a service to your media job and improve your own position in it. No matter what your job, your ability to take complex matters and put them into words and phrases that are readily understood, makes you a communicator.

"I cannot emphasize enough the importance of learning to be self-sufficient," says Bob DeLay, President of the Direct Mail/Marketing Association. "Young people go out looking for jobs today, and too often, they have been given an unrealistic idea of what to expect. They think it's going to be much easier than it is. In today's marketplace, it is a very aggressive and competitive environment. You should be self-sufficient. You should be able to solve problems yourself. One of the ways you can do this at the entry level is to find out *exactly* what simple skills you might need in order to be able to participate in the field of your desire. For example, in public relations, you should at least know how to write a press release."

Bernice Grossman agrees. "You'd be surprised at how many

people I interview who don't even know that there are three basic areas of magazine publishing (advertising, editorial, and circulation)."

WHAT KIND OF JOB DO YOU WANT AND CAN YOU DO?

Start by finding out about the medium or media which hold appeal for you. Is it the subject matter that you like, or the chance to use your own capabilities and interests? There's an important difference. If your personal qualities are the main route by which you fit into a career, then be thinking of ways to apply those elements you possess.

Consider your capabilities: some came naturally, while others were acquired. Through education and the passage of time, you learned many facts and ways to approach problems. You have often been reminded that education teaches you how to think, regardless of the subject matter. But thinking is not a skill which employers are considering while trying to fill an entry-level or lower-level job. That is why there is a greater need to have taken specific courses that will help you launch your career. More and more jobs have become specialized and technical. As a former commissioner of education said, "To send young men and women into today's world armed only with Aristotle, Freud, and Hemingway is like sending a lamb into a lion's den." So, if you've gone to school and studied literature, and don't know anything about art (and that's what you want to do), even if you are talented, it's essential that you get that background.

"It is important to have some kind of management courses as part of your background," John Pahmer, New York marketing consultant, feels. "If not, then it is important to go out and take a course—at night school, or in the daytime, if time allows—and get some hands-on project management experience," he continues. "This means that you should be able to coordinate a project. Since you usually get this experience on the job, and if you have not had any kind of previous experience where you could conceivably have gotten project management experience, then I would suggest doing some kind of volunteer work."

Then, you should consider all the things you might be able to do: to write, relate to people, to investigate, to speak convincingly, to photograph, to draw, *to apply determination to whatever you tackle.* These, and a wealth of other possible qualities, can fit into many places. Even though you should be more than willing (and happy, too) to work at almost anything in your chosen field, try first for a job that trains you, or actually places you, in a function that the organization depends on. This might be as a marketing trainee, an administrative assistant to an executive with important duties, or in any job whose tasks put you right up on the front line.

Be careful of jobs that are so highly specialized that advancement is difficult. For example, there is a highly competent librarian in a corporate library who works with all forms of information coming from books, reports, magazines, and even computerized data supplied by outside firms. But is there a chance for her to move up, out of the library? Not unless she really works at it—and it may mean a down step (something employees are often reluctant to take). Despite a good salary, she's now locked in. Skills at market research and knowing where to obtain important answers for selling the company's existing or potential products are her background, but she let herself be boxed into a job. A recent study said that ninety per cent of job-holders are so afraid of losing their jobs or of speaking up courageously and constructively, that they really don't make the best use of their potential. And that's an important point. *Don't be afraid to speak up, to ask questions.* Not only does it show an interest on your part, but it can open up new areas of opportunities.

"I'm convinced that I got my first promotion not only because of my ability to do a good job," states Alex Gotfryd, now Vice-President and Art Director of Doubleday & Company, "but also because I did not hesitate to express my opinion. Taking initiative and not being afraid to say what you think is a very important factor to success and advancement in business. The secret, of course, is saying what you mean in a subtle and tactful way that does not offend other people."

So as you read the next chapter about specific media fields

and their jobs, keep an eye on the future. Take an entry-level
job to get started and become trained, but remember, it's up to
you to make something out of it. You're out to build a career
for yourself which gives satisfaction and monetary rewards, so
always keep the overall picture in mind while dealing with in-
terim duties and details.

TOUGH COMPETITION AND THE ENTRY-LEVEL JOB

In job hunting, it is absolutely essential to remember that the
competition is tough, and that your main objective is to get a
job in the field you want. And many times, that can mean almost any job. One of the biggest mistakes that young people
make is thinking that many jobs are just not good enough for
them with their education.

"My advice to people who want to get into the media business," says the Development Manager of a major publishing
company, "is to become a secretary. In this way you can see all
the facets of the business. And if you can't be a secretary, then
get in any way you can. Don't feel that because you have a degree that secretarial or clerical work is demeaning. There is no
substitute for on-the-job training.

"At our company," this executive continues, "we have a Career Opportunities Program, which means that all openings in
the company are posted so that once you have been here for
ten months, you can try for another position. But if you didn't
work here, you might never have that opportunity with an outside recruiter."

"Don't look down on any type of job at the outset. You may
not be thrilled to tell your friends you are a secretary after four
years of college," says Jane Wolchonok, Marketing Manager at
Citibank, "but you learn how an office works and what kind of
opportunities there are for you. Besides, it's so much easier to
get into something from the inside. Many people think a lot of
jobs are beneath them when it really depends on you and how
resourceful you are."

It's great to start as assistant manager of a company because
you have an MBA, and become president in a few years. But it

doesn't happen that way, unless your dad owns the business . . . and even then, it probably will not occur.

Suppose you can only get a job as a secretary, despite your degree, job experience, and obvious talents of many types. Certainly you can get bored being a gofer (be it going for coffee or shopping for presents for the boss). Straight routine typing is no fun. But what are the benefits? Some might be:

- Getting to learn your department, inside out.

- Finding out who runs what, who has power, and using that information to help prepare for your own forward motion.

- Possessing a Who's Who in your mind of people inside and outside the company soon starts paying dividends. You can talk to them, exchange news and rumors, and learn facts which can become handy in many ways.

- Not letting questions go by without finding out the answers. The boss and others love to teach you. Everyone benefits, and you learn a lot.

- Patience and loyalty will be appreciated. It improves the chances of "luck" bringing benefits your way, when you are in the right place at the right time.

- Being known, and knowing your job, thus decreasing future training needed in the company. It opens opportunities in the organization. It is easier for an executive to arrange a promotion or transfer in order to get the right person by selecting someone already known. You are the person known. Besides, it is a lot of work breaking in an unknown outsider, rather than selecting a trained or capable person already on staff.

- Being flexible in fitting your hours and tasks to the needs of the boss. Even if inconvenient, it gives you an entrée to the "in" crowd, which might not occur if you remained wedded to routine hours and a fixed work pattern. Executives are more likely to give preference and opportunities to flexible, reliable, capable helpers and associates.

- Sharing the work of your boss, if you are a secretary or

administrative assistant. You don't have the boss's title, but you are the "ear" of the person for whom you work and an extension of his or her power. So instead of being a slave to a routine, you are an executive-in-training. When you can do all the jobs without asking a lot of questions, you are probably ready to move up the next step in pay and position.

● Learning who is important and who isn't; who is worth cultivating for friendship and favors, and who isn't likely to matter too much.

● Possibly receiving time off for additional training, or payment for attending outside courses. The purpose is to train you to do better on your job and prepare you to move up. Better to be paid for education and training with the company's blessings, rather than taking cash out of your own pocket!

There are more benefits, for sure, in any job. Your *outlook and willingness are what count,* along with your personal capability to relate to the company world around you. By showing optimism and displaying willingness, avenues of opportunity can open up to you that don't usually occur through normal channels. The full reality of what on-the-job experience will teach you is not spelled out in classroom studies or newspaper advertisements for employment.

In essence, an entry-level job opens a multitude of ways to self-advertise within the company. It lets executives know that you are a capable individual. The next time there is a good job available, you come to mind. It is easier to promote somebody in the company, than search for replacements of unknown quality from outside sources.

"Whether it's entry into the business as a secretary or in the mailroom," says John Pahmer, a New York marketing consultant, "nowadays you can make almost anything out of any job. The trick is not to stay there for so long that you get stereotyped into that position."

Don't ever dismiss the value of starting at the bottom. It can provide you with a lot of basic information. For example, if you worked in the mailroom, you'd learn the insurance protection provided for advertising plates sent via United Parcel. Or, if you had to rush 150 pounds of books in a crate via Greyhound's N.B.O. (Next Bus Out) service from your New York office to Montreal, you'd know it could be done. The mailroom can provide valuable training and opportunities, including a chance to find out what positions are becoming available within the company.

It really doesn't matter where you start. With your next position, you'll have some kind of a choice. And at that time, make sure it is in an area you want to be and that it will give you an opportunity to meet the decision makers. "Get near the decision makers," says Thomas Moore, President of Tomorrow Entertainment, Inc., "make contact with them and develop as much contact with them through conversations as you can. You'll get a lot better experience working around the decision makers, too."

Another point to keep in mind, is that at any point in your life it is possible that you will make a major change in your work. Read the biographies of people in the media, or glance at some of the *Who's Who* listings of various people. Few have stayed in the same company, and many have made radical changes in jobs held. So just make the best choices you can in your career drive. Don't berate yourself if you find reason to change direction from time to time. It's normal, and not a sign of a wrong choice that nobody else would have made. There are recourses to take in the job areas you consider, and in your assigned duties once you get on a payroll. You aren't a helpless victim of the circumstances that put you where you are, nor are you powerless to alter your future.

YOU NEVER KNOW . . .

You never know what is going to get you into a media profession. For example, during the early 1950s, a young graduate in literature opened a dressmaking business with two helpers, in a room above a noodle restaurant six subway stops from the famous Ginza area of Tokyo, Japan. One day a Japanese motion picture producer, shopping in the area, noticed one of her dresses on a mannequin in the shop window. He commissioned her to design costumes for a movie. That led to work on some 600 pictures in the following years, plus personal orders from leading actresses in Japan. Prosperity helped her firm grow. Today, this woman is world famous. Her name? Hanae Mori.

Today, Hanae Mori has more than fifteen companies bearing her name, designing and manufacturing fashion items ranging from high-style evening gowns to bed sheets and bath towels. Factories and stores are located around the world. She has now made an arrangement to begin a joint publishing venture with New York's Fairchild Publications by starting *Tokyo Women's Wear Daily*. If the publication lives up to the prestigious New York version, upon which the U.S. fashion industry depends, she will be in as glamorous a media career as many people could desire, not even counting her other involvements. So, to prove a point about getting into media, you don't necessarily have to move from being a literature graduate directly into a publishing office to make a success in publishing!

However, equally as important, you can't leave your career to chance. The purpose of this book is to assist you in the careful planning that can help you to achieve this kind of success without leaving it up to fate!

Chapter 2

BASICS YOU SHOULD KNOW ABOUT THE PROFESSIONS: THE INDUSTRIES AND THE JOBS IN THEM

THE INDUSTRIES

Within each mode of communication, there are many tasks to be performed. To find out more about them, begin by exploring some of the realms of the media to see what kinds of jobs there are, and the type of work involved. The further you get into each one, the more possibilities and directions you will discover. All this will help you to become more specific in your job search and to know a good opportunity when you see it.

PUBLISHING

Books   In the United States about 45,000 different books are produced each year. Publishers vary in size from producers of one or two books a year, up to major firms having many divisions, each responsible for hundreds of different books (referred to as "titles" in the trade). Products can vary from an ultra-high quality full-color coffee-table book to a multivolume set of encyclopedias, or from a 480-page novel to a 96-page specialty report of interest to a limited audience. Physical appearance can be hardcover or paperback, pocket-size or over-size. Each choice of presentation, text, illustration, physical form, and quantity to be printed depends on a wide variety of decisions made by people in many roles. Your position, in a publishing firm, can affect those decisions.

Those decision-making roles often start with the editorial department, in which there are duties similar in many respects to those in newspaper and magazine publishing. If you seek a job in this area, there are writers (both staff and freelance), artists (both staff and freelance), copy editors, acquisitions (purchasing) editors, and various levels of editors with other responsibilities. Also included are editorial assistants, researchers, proofreaders, graphic designers, and junior roles in relation to any of these jobs.

The production departments make a physical reality of the books, usually by coordinating the work of outside organizations such as typesetters, printers, binders, paper merchants, and transport companies. The sales department activities are based on the firm's products, using staff and independent representatives, plus having varying degrees of involvement in advertising, publicity, and the many alternate routes that can be taken to keep sales moving.

The selling or obtaining of rights to material controlled by a publisher is in the domain of the rights and permissions department. The business department personnel keep track of costs, budgets, payrolls, royalties, and other accounting activities, while they also determine whether projects are profitable and give approval on the editorial and other departments' projected expenses. There are a wide variety of jobs, so your direction can be quite diverse.

In the supporting roles of book publishing are many freelance and independent firms. Some "package" books for others, by providing all or part of the steps toward getting a book ready to be sold. Others do design, writing, promotion, publicity, proofreading . . . the area is filled with tasks that publishers often find better to subcontract to others. (Some of the many types of jobs are more fully described later in this chapter.)

Magazines   Generally, this term covers any publication for home readership, other than newspapers. Of the approximately 10,000 different magazines in the United States, about 175 are daily, almost 2,000 weekly or several times a month, about 4,000 monthlies, and the rest with other frequencies. Canadian publications are about nine per cent of this figure, and also nine per cent of the newspaper totals. *Ulrich's International Periodicals Directory* lists 62,000 world-wide.

Some magazines are high-gloss, gloriously full-color periodicals in magazine or book format, while others are on newsprint and in black ink only, and still others are newspaperlike in appearance, but devoted to special interests. *Ayer's Directory* breaks the editorial-interest areas into nearly 900 classifications. Name any subject, interest, or geographical area, and you'll find at least one periodical aimed for that market. Just starting down the list, there are periodicals involved with abrasives, accident prevention, accountants, acoustics, adventure, advertising, aeronautics, agents, agnostics, agriculture, agricultural implements, air conditioning . . . the list spans the alphabet.

All of these periodicals need the same type of personnel as newspapers—writers, editors, sometimes photographers, usually an advertising staff, circulation department people, production, art, and business department staff—and often require specialists who are not on a newspaper's staff. An example is *Consumer Reports*, a magazine that publishes the findings of their large staff. Based on the assessments of the staff's specialists, the reader can consult the magazine to see which products to purchase and which to avoid. Many magazines have gone into spin-off activities, or other publishing areas, producing books, pamphlets, newsletters, and other products.

Magazines have their deadlines and production needs, just as newspapers do, but they vary with every periodical. Most magazines do not have their own printing facilities, but all editorial requirements call for capable staffs. While a few magazines rely solely on staff output, many use freelance material and this, by the way, can be a great way to get experience.

"Freelance work can lead to all sorts of things," believes an associate editor at Simon & Schuster. "Don't wait for a full-time job. Even while you're actively looking, you can seek out freelance. A little experience can go a long way." Though it's a rare beginner who can hunt down substantial amounts of freelance work, it does count strongly in your favor if you get any kind of freelance experience.

Many magazines will take entry-level graduates, and your chances are greatly enhanced if you have familiarity with the subject matter of the publication. (See *Writer's Market,* or its companion monthly magazine, for additional information.)

NEWSLETTERS   This is a big and growing area. Instead of a monthly magazine filled with lengthy editorial pieces and a wealth of advertising, there is a growing need for the newsletter's specialized report of the latest news regarding an industry or special subject. Usually, they are a few pages in length, go out first-class mail, carry no advertising, have a limited number of readers, and are often sold by subscription at a fairly high price. Based on frequency, subject matter and importance to the reader, prices might range from $10 a year up to $20,000. (The latter figure would be for a technical report—it would typically report on a development before it is announced to the trade or general press—bought by companies who want to know what's pending with their competitors.)

Becoming associated with a newsletter usually calls for knowledge of the subject matter in which the publication deals. From time to time, various supporting staff jobs open up, providing the training and knowledge that enables people to become adept at seeking and communicating collected data.

Newspapers   Just in the United States alone, there are about 10,000 newspapers of the general news type. This doesn't count those aimed at trade or specialized readerships. Among general-readership newspapers there are about 1,700 dailies, 65 triweeklies, more than 500 twice-weeklies, in excess of 7,000 weeklies, and another hundred or so at twice-monthly, monthly, or bimonthly frequency. For a list of all of them, with details about circulation, location, frequency, editor, address and staff, look at publications such as *Ayer's Directory,* and the annual compendiums of *Editor and Publisher* magazine, along with further information in *Standard Rate and Data Service*'s section on newspapers. Most libraries have at least one of these publications.

More than 40,000 reporters are employed by newspapers, the great majority in medium-sized towns. There is a great turnover rate, but by the same token, there are many more applicants waiting in the wings than can be absorbed. More than 90 colleges and universities offer master's or doctorate degrees in journalism. To this, add the more than 250 colleges with undergraduate journalism training, and an additional 500 junior colleges. Newspapers cannot hire every job-seeker as a reporter, and you may want to consider other areas of newspaper employment. There are almost 400,000 people on newspaper payrolls, and reporters are just ten per cent of that total. Many journalism graduates are trained in the business and advertising side of newspapers, as well as in circulation, so these job areas might be worth your consideration.

Journalism training includes copyreading, reporting, editing, feature writing, and often law. Most editors selecting newcomers prefer those with a liberal arts background, and more preferably, those who have had some kind of journalism exposure in addition.

Most reporters start on weekly or small daily publications (where they may even double as a photographer). According to one old newspaper hand, ideal editorial department qualities include a "nose for news, curiosity, persistence, initiative, resourcefulness, an accurate memory, and the ability to handle the fast-paced life and deadlines." Large dailies generally require several years' editorial experience before accepting applicants.

Experienced reporters may get such desirable assignments as editorial writers, correspondents in distant locations, columnists, and department editorships. Newspaper training is a typical starting point for related writing fields, such as in magazine work, public relations, and preparing material for radio and television news programs. It also readies people for advertising, technical publishing, and working in the communications department of private companies.

ADVERTISING/MARKETING

Every business and service needs ways to persuade people to come to them, to spend or give money. Advertising does this in many ways and through numerous routes. The talents, variety of tasks to fulfill and objectives are many.

Start by considering skills provided by creative professionals: writers, artists, designers, and photographers. Add to them the work of other specialists who find out whether there is a market for a certain business, product, or service. Then decide how best to create a preference that helps the advertiser attract the desired results. Now other people get involved in deciding which medium is the best choice. Avenues might be via radio, television, billboards, issuing catalogs, placing advertisements in magazines or newspapers, mailing literature directly to likely prospects, arranging for the delivery of supporting information such as in brochures and flyers, and producing sound and/or visual means to communicate information. Elements contributing to company identification through packaging and design play a significant role, such as Kodak's use of yellow in its ads and on its boxes, the big "M" used by McDonald's food stores, and the racing greyhound of the Greyhound buses and services.

Jobs in advertising and marketing are essential to selling, so their growth rate is faster than that of most other occupations. Most employers prefer college graduates, especially those who have emphasized marketing, business, or journalism in their training. Others make their selections using different criteria. Often some work-related experience in school publications, school broadcasting, or from a summer job can give the needed edge.

"I have a golden rule that I've always worked by," Bob DeLay of the Direct Mail/Marketing Association says, "and it is simply this: Who, What, Where, When and How? Be able to answer these questions on the basics of any field in which you are interested. And be able to answer, at least in part, these questions about the employer you are hoping to work for. It's one way of giving yourself a competitive edge.

"Another suggestion I would make to anyone getting into business is to find a way to learn about business before you work," Bob DeLay continues. "In other words, learn how to make money pay off. Understand what it means so that you are not utilizing just theory that you may have learned in school. I would do this even if it means doing volunteer work."

Hiring is done by numerous groups: advertising and marketing agencies, private employers, broadcasters, publishers, nonprofit organizations, and many firms which provide supporting services to these groups.

Advertising is an area in which you can usually expect to work under pressure, possibly change jobs a number of times, and lack the security found in many other occupations. You are expected to produce high-quality results in a short time. Long or irregular hours to meet promises and deadlines are normal. Expect last-minute changes which put the squeeze on everyone down the line. A minor change of one word in an advertisement ready for the press may cause a chain reaction of considerable expense and investment of time. The account executive rushes to the art department to alter the layout, the art department's changes cause overtime with the typesetters, the typesetters' changes mean a remake of the color separation negatives, which in turn necessitates the making of a new printing plate.

Advertising and marketing can provide exciting and satisfying careers for anyone who enjoys variety, creative challenges, problems to be solved, and survives the competition coming from other persons and companies competing for the same account.

PUBLIC RELATIONS

There is an important need to improve understanding and foster cooperation among individuals, organizations and institutions. Each person or group needs to make its views known, to portray them in the most desirable fashion possible, and to do their best to have their views well received by others. That communications task is the domain of public relations.

P.R. is a two-directional job. It seeks to spread the good word, yet it is the same channel that gathers the information telling how the individual or organization is viewed by others. The task of public relations personnel is to be the route through which information is taken in, processed, and presented anew.

Routes for communicating and the methods employed have to be imaginative and diverse. Well over 100,000 people have full-time jobs in P.R., representing business firms, public utilities, trade and professional groups, colleges, museums, religious institutions, human-service organizations, health and medical groups, government agencies, individuals, and a host of others needing to let the world know of their works and needs. For example, if a company receives a complaint that is hard to handle or seems unreasonable, there are ways for the company to keep a good relationship with the complainant and avoid turning him/her off. Skill is required in knowing how to build and maintain a positive public reputation.

Public relations workers have to be able to gather information, write, speak, and deal effectively with people. Creativity, initiative and the ability to express thoughts clearly and simply are important. Most valuable is an outgoing personality, self-confidence, understanding of human psychology, and an ability to "think on your feet," especially when unexpected situations develop, or an embarrassing event has to be down-played or placed in a more favorable light. Initiating and writing pamphlets to distribute to the public or interested parties is another duty of P.R., along with writing press releases and issuing newsworthy photographs. The free space such releases obtain often far surpasses in impact paid advertising by the same organization.

The tendency to split advertising from public relations has increased in recent years. Both have their own ways of communicating their messages. Some businesses or groups consider public relations a mode of obtaining inexpensive advertising. Yet in this capacity there is a limit to how far P.R. can take the company. At other times, public relations is a way of establishing a positive impression about products that may be difficult to achieve with ads. Part of the public relations person's job is to develop new ideas and approaches continually, since old or routine methods can fail to grab attention. The objective is to pick the image and goal you desire to reach, and try to make a reality of it in the minds of others. People, companies, and groups may have need for your product and services, but the mode of reaching and convincing them can be quite diverse.

Some of the ways of communicating include announcements

of events that get space in newspapers and magazines, as well as mention on radio and television. Often, public relations personnel supply or encourage various media executives to assign people to photograph, write about, or broadcast the event. Sometimes the task may be to provide a speaker and write the speech to be given, arrange "how-to" demonstrations, send representatives on tour, provide materials or speakers to civic and business groups, or supply information or materials to schools.

Getting involved in community activities brings the names and objectives of individuals, groups, and companies to public notice, and, if done effectively, implants the image and message desired. Publicity in trade publications plays a large role for some companies and organizations. The space occupied by such information can be worth many dollars, if measured in terms of what the space would cost as paid advertising.

Other public relations techniques for gaining publicity include such things as open houses, plant tours, anniversary celebrations, conventions, displays, contests, small gifts, remembrance-advertising items, and even samples of products. Parties held for members of the media, to make announcements or show new products or facilities, are also in the public relations area.

Many of the jobs described later in this chapter would give you a place on a public relations staff. The fact that there are other types of duties is obvious, based on the needs involved. Projects call for continual variety and attention-getting devices.

Competition for beginning jobs is keen. Public relations work has an aura of glamour and excitement that attracts large numbers of job-seekers. In addition, many people transfer to this work from other media jobs. Yet there are always openings that occur. Most of the jobs which become available will be with large organizations, private companies, public relations firms, educational institutions, public utilities, fund-raising groups, and often the government.

Radio and Television Broadcasting and Cable Systems

The business of radio and television is vast. There are almost 7,500 commercial radio stations, and 750 commercial TV stations. Add the public broadcasting group and you increase the radio figure by almost 1,000 and the television stations by approximately 300. Then add to these totals about 4,000 cable television systems.

The number of both radio and TV stations is on the verge of expanding appreciably. Present radio frequency widths are likely to be narrowed, to create space for more broadcasters. In television, because of the weak broadcasting signal of UHF stations, Channels 14 to 83 were generally ignored and almost unsalable until a few years ago. Now, with the advent of cable, UHF stations are delivered as clearly as VHF (Channels 2 to 13), and their values are often in the multimillion dollar range. The growth explosion of radio and cable television is similar to that of FM radio two decades earlier. This is not only a boon to radio and TV program syndication, but also opens the way for many new job openings to fulfill programming, production, technical, and sales needs.

On UHF, during lean times, programs were kept alive with foreign language schedules, religious broadcasts, sports, children's shows, and business news, plus commercial and documentary films obtained at little or no cost. Now their shows are broadening and generating purchase by becoming ingenious in local programming and holding the viewers' attention with retransmission of regular radio and TV material. Major broadcasting groups and publishers are getting deeply interested in cable, and financially involved. As licenses are gradually issued, subscription television has added new products and opportunities.

How dependent are the programs and types of workers needed by television stations, film, or program-producing independents on the people who watch the shows? By the time a student graduates from high school, about 18,000 hours will have been spent in front of the video tube, as compared with 12,000 hours in the classroom! So, name the subject, and there is the need for a program and the people to make it.

Radio stations specialize, based on their target audiences. Surveys indicate to advertisers which broadcasters are reaching their audience most effectively and it is to these broadcasters that the advertising money generally flows. Companies seek to get the broadest audience for the sale of their products and services, so it is essential to be in the top three stations, in some areas, to attract these ads. Some stations do best by specializing in disco or rock music, some in country and western, while other stations feature talk and information. Still others play only music, or solely broadcast news; stations continually pick the directions which they feel will pay off. The challenge of improving listener-ratings creates the need for personnel who can make it possible, which in turn provides opportunities for new talent and creative efforts.

See such reference manuals as *Broadcasting Yearbook,* that has a listing of all radio (and television) stations, and a wealth of information associated with any firm or activity which has a role in the broadcasting industry.

In radio, the average station has 11 full-time workers and 4 part-time. Smaller stations survive with only 4 or 5 people; larger ones in major cities may have more than 100 employees. A typical small TV station might have 30 people, while major metropolitan stations employ up to 250 or even more. The amount of material picked up from seven national radio networks, regional networks, and three major national television networks, affects the figures. The three major national television networks alone employ almost 15,000 workers, with an enormous variety of jobs to be done.

Traditionally, broadcast stations have four major departments: programming, engineering, sales, and administration. The larger the station, the more the jobs become divided. For instance, in programming, news activities are often split off from other programs and made into a separate department. The station's size makes a difference. Small radio stations prefer to have as many staff members as possible be legally qualified to operate transmitters, and you can end up announcing, writing, selling, or operating the control board. Whatever the job, you'll get a valuable education in such a setting, and be paid, rather than being billed by a school for related information. Experience of this nature on your record, plus the contacts you make, can open avenues and doors normally not available in a large organization that has structured boundaries.

Staff members are responsible for daily and weekly shows. Each has an assignment, is appointed to cover certain types of events, or be responsible for other elements in producing the shows. Freelance performers, writers, singers, and other entertainers are often hired for specific broadcasts or series. The station's programming also depends on the extent to which its broadcasts are live, recorded, syndicated, or received from networks.

Some of the programming department's jobs are described later in this chapter. Duties in the engineering department are learned either through technical school training or acquired on the job. This might include positioning of microphones, adjusting sound levels, doing lighting, operating cameras, and working with electric and electronic equipment. These tasks often require union membership. Similarly, in the sales department, there are many steps that require a large number of skills, an outlook, knowledge, and experience gained through acquiring a bachelor's degree, or even an MBA. Financial rewards in selling, as in many sales jobs elsewhere, can often be *far* better than other jobs in the same organization.

"Radio sales, especially, offers young people, even at the entry level, a great opportunity to make a lot of money, and eventually, if they're good enough, to move into management," says Robert Silverman, Chairman of the Board of a New York metropolitan area radio station.

"The highest paid job on most stations is generally sales," Bob continues. "Most people think it's the on-the-air personality who gets all the money, but it's simply not true. In fact, when you stop to think, it is really the sales person who is the greatest talent, because he or she is the one who produces the money that supports the station."

THE JOBS

Although the mass media fields are all very different, many of the jobs available use the same talents and almost the same background. If you ever want to switch laterally to another company, or move into another industry, much of your training and work-experience will be valuable. For your reference, here are a few specific types of jobs. Many wouldn't be handed to you upon entering, but you could easily find yourself being edged into their responsibilities before long. So, remember, taking one type of job doesn't freeze your movement into another, once you get a start.

PUBLISHING

No matter what you do or where you go, writing is likely to be part of your work. The better you do it, the more promising the market for your services. Knowing how to write an effective business letter, send announcements about a company's products, prepare a report, draft copy for an advertisement, write text for a mail-order catalog, type out instructions, or rewrite somebody else's material—all these capabilities can be used or transferred as you progress. If you can write on one subject, you can learn to write on another subject fairly quickly.

Some occupations require writing abilities that incorporate knowledge or other training, such as economics, history, electronics, agriculture, music, automobiles, medicine, or a wealth of other subjects. Many types of media can utilize this knowledge and writing ability, enabling you to switch easily from advertising to magazine articles to preparing a book for publication. Familiarity with art, for instance, helped one art history graduate move up from unwrapping old lamps for sale in an auction gallery to being in charge of publications and high-priced catalogs for a major international auction firm.

In this instance, a liberal arts student found a home and use for his training in an unexpected way and in a medium he had not originally envisioned. So if you want to be a writer, keep in mind that there are many ways to find use for your talents. Here are a few of the most common publishing jobs.

Editorial

EDITORIAL ASSISTANT   Look in any big-city newspaper in a publishing center, or in publishing trade journals, and you may find an ad for "editorial assistant." Employment agencies advertise these positions or have such jobs on file. In publishing, especially books and trade magazines, being an editorial secretary or assistant is a very sought after starting position. Part of your responsibilities may include proofreading, research, replying to authors' inquiries, coordinating production schedules, or doing any number of chores that you think are below your educational and personal capabilities. They may be, but if they are part of the job, someone has to do them. And yet, these are the fundamental duties which you will depend on as you climb the ladder. *It's really a training program—accept it as such.* Before long, you'll be asked to give your opinion, to read manuscripts, write headlines or copy, and gradually take on more duties that the editor feels comfortable in shifting over to you. It is in a job like this that you'll get used to meeting deadlines, working under pressure, taking orders, and learning how to give instructions or deal with people tactfully.

"One thing I'm *not* interested in is people who tell you upfront that there are certain things they will and won't do," Bernice Grossman of *Co-ed* magazine states emphatically. "If someone is looking for advancement, that's fine. I'm happy to help them along. But first, they've got to fill the responsibilities of the job that is open."

WRITER   Unless you're a freelancer, which is rare (and most difficult) for beginners, most of the material you'll encounter is likely to be nonfiction. Subject matter based on specific assignments from a publisher or advertiser will orient your direction. You may elect to freelance to get a start, or make it your career. Some assignments can be for a stipulated fee if freelance, or done as a staff assignment. In such cases, you'll conduct research, make notes to retain your ideas and observations, and seek information or details from others. Your style of writing, subjects in which you have gained specialized knowledge, the markets that use your writing, and subject matter assigned are what determine your direction. Within this area, there can be a wide range of challenges to prove your capabilities to yourself and to others.

"A writer is a temporary expert on any subject to which his attention is turned, based on the assignment or project," says Joe Scott, author of more than twenty nonfiction books. "For example, my wife and I wrote a book on Egyptian hieroglyphs," he continues, "with no special training or knowledge on the subject. By the time we had researched it, studied the subject and traveled to Egypt for more knowledge, we were 'experts.' In fact, the curator at the Cairo Museum was so impressed with our manuscript that he wrote the foreword for the book!"

COPYWRITER   There is always a need for advertising copy to be used in publications, broadcasting, or for private company use. Words also take an important place in brochures, mail-order literature, and flyers. The style, length of text, and editorial approach come from conferences with managers, the artist involved, the size of the printed piece, and technical details that let you know what is wanted. Research and interviews for information are part of your job. To do the best work, you will want to keep abreast of advertising trends, marketing surveys, competitive products, and the work of other companies. Part of your duties could include writing articles, bulletins, sales letters, speeches, promotional material, and text for in-house publications.

"One of the most challenging things about copywriting is that there are certain constraints within which copywriters must work. For instance, you have got to take into consideration the size of the ad you are working with, the method by which it will be reproduced, the budget limitations of the client, the deadline —a whole lot more than just the message that the client and the agency want to get across. But whatever you do, you have still got to write material that will sell," says Druanne Dillon, copywriter at Zimmermann Marketing, Inc.

Editorial in Publishing and Broadcasting

REPORTER   The ability to have a "nose for news," gather it, analyze it, and write articles is used throughout publishing, be it newspapers, magazines, radio, television, company publications, or newsletters. You'll work on assignments, or pursue your own leads and be responsible for covering certain types of information. In small newspapers and on some trade publications, especially when on a trip away from the office, you may be taking photographs too. Reporters for radio or television need to have verbal ability, to be able to give live reports on events as they happen. From general reporting, you may go into specialties such as sports, police, court trials, politics or other areas. With news services or larger communications firms, assignments may be to distant or even foreign locations. These duties come after gaining local experience and training.

NEWSWRITER   On a newspaper this is sometimes called "Rewrite." Material is received from reporters, be it one reporter or several, and from the various other sources including information gathered from the files, interviews, and phone calls. You must package the information into a single story or feature. An additional responsibility concerns verifying facts, and research for additional information, when a story from a reporter or other source requires such follow-through.

READER   When articles or stories arrive, the reader studies them, analyzes the subject matter, and makes recommendations to the editor. This involves whether or not to buy, whether to change the whole focus or make minor alterations.

TECHNICAL WRITER   In such a role, you could work for a newspaper, magazine, book publisher, broadcasting station, the government, or a private company. The technical writer develops, writes, and edits material of many types. Text comes from research, interviews, and actual hands-on experience using the product. Valuable assets for such a job include being good at detail, being interested in finding out how things work, and being able to translate technical or complex information into easy-to-understand language.

EDITOR   There are all types of editors, based on the areas and scope of responsibility. With a title such as this, you will usually have others working for you. You'll select which materials are to be published, broadcast, or photographed. The editor plans, arranges material, rewrites, verifies, compiles, cuts, abstracts, or makes changes according to personal or specified viewpoints. The editor coordinates the work of authors, designers, production personnel, printers, and other associates. Some editors specialize in certain subjects or branches of expertise. If you are just entering the media world, you will have to work your way into the responsibilities of editor, rather than have them assigned quickly.

Art and Design   Anyone concerned with designing and executing artwork is included in an important area of communicating ideas and visual images which affect acceptance of the product or service involved. Many of the art areas are directly related to media. Other artwork is in realms which influence the media's ability to communicate, but do not directly work for a publisher, broadcaster, advertiser or film producer. For instance, is the interior designer of room-setting and color use, working in media when full-color sketches are made from which others will form opinions, spend money, and make a reality in the manufacturing processes? Such a job exists in numerous home-making publications, such as *House & Garden, Better Homes & Gardens,* or *McCall's,* in which the illustrations are actually produced, or a room is furnished to fit the interior designer's illustration.

COMMERCIAL ARTIST   As an artist, you can indicate that you can do, or are familiar with, almost anything requiring visual, artistic communication. As a media artist you may be asked to do illustrations, designs, layouts, or, just as likely, paste-ups ready for camera. The opportunities are good if you have the ability, the creativity, and can get into a spot which lets you get started. Even if you narrow down your field to certain areas, like doing advertising layouts or preparing camera-ready mechanicals, there is plenty of work in that area alone. Within the media industries, artists can be assigned to editorial

units, to advertising departments, or to special departments that
handle a variety of assignments. Within nonmedia companies,
you can be preparing catalogs, brochures, presentations, billboard art, or even painting signs.

Then too, as a commercial artist, there is a wealth of specialties which you may gravitate to, including fashion, display,
print, direct mail, technical specialties, product illustrations,
and a host of other groups. Since artists work in many media,
and have a wide scope of techniques and materials, the term
"artist" is a general title. Narrow down the areas in which you
want to work.

"Set up a goal for yourself and constantly work towards it,"
states Alex Gotfryd, Vice-President and Art Director of Doubleday & Company. "Prepare a portfolio especially geared to the
field in which you want to work."

Unlike other media job seekers, the artist should avoid following the recommendation to "get a foot in the door," by taking any job, even as a mailroom clerk or secretary. That kind of
job is not likely to put you any closer to getting a start in art,
unless it is a position specifically within the art department.

ILLUSTRATOR   In this type of work, you can move in such
realms as fashion, graphic design, cartoons, quick-sketches, advertising illustrations, layouts, portraits, or pictorial settings.
Specializing in certain subject matter can also orient you toward medicine, science, mechanics, maps, lettering, logotypes,
furniture, clothing, people, architecture, nature settings, plants,
animals, and many other items. Many illustrations are bought
from freelance artists. The amount of work for you in freelance
can be just as great, the income possibly higher than that of a
staff job, and working conditions will be more under your own
control. It may be necessary to approach an artists' representative to sell your work effectively to places not readily
accessible to you. For this service, the representative receives a
commission based on the amount of the sale.

PHOTOGRAPHER   It has been said that eighty-five per cent of
what you learn is perceived through your eyes. Photographs
play an important role in communicating information to be ab-

sorbed. This includes all types of photos, whether still or in motion, on film or video-tape, or through electronic means. It can involve people, animals, events, news, history, use of products, teaching, showing buildings and geographical settings—in short, almost anything. And how impressively you communicate images with your equipment is a measurement of the future you can carve out for yourself.

Photography can fit normal media uses as well as a spectrum of specific applications. A friend of mine on the staff of a major bank receives a variety of assignments that require industrial photos for an annual report. One day it's shooting a fire truck (financed by the bank) at the scene of a burning building, the next it's photographing New York City and the harbor from the air, and another day it's putting together a display of photographs showing interesting people and scenes taken at branch banks. The photos are used in news media, public relations work, records, company sales and training departments, and a number of them for advertising, be it a print ad or bank display.

Involvement in photography includes a lot more than just operating a camera. It includes all the supporting roles as well. This might be planning what is to be photographed, choosing settings, preparing the subjects, taking light levels, processing films and prints, selecting photographs from files, or being in charge of recording names and events displayed in the pictures. These roles, at any time, can cause a person to move sideways or upward in order to fill a need.

Apprenticeships are abundant in photography. It's possible for a darkroom assistant to be called upon to take an assignment or become assignment director for the other photographers. Managerial roles develop from experience gained; your ability to make decisions, show initiative, display ingenuity, and be self-motivating will be noticed and rewarded. A career enabling you to move up the photographic-department ladder can be stimulating and worthwhile. But remember, don't be too disturbed at getting the more menial tasks or assignments at first, as long as it is a start in gaining your objective.

ADVERTISING/MARKETING AND PUBLIC RELATIONS

The scope of occupations and specialties that spread the news about products, services and ideas is enormous.

Advertising agencies have swung more heavily into marketing in the past decade, rather than just preparing and executing campaigns for the various media (print, broadcast, direct mail, etc.). Entire programs of sales, catalogs, distribution, supporting literature, product design, company image, price levels, and related subjects are involved. So marketing, as such, is but a part of what you will encounter; advertising is only one of the routes involved in making a sale and must be supported by many levels of observations, decisions, and follow-up.

As opposed to other media jobs, in an advertising/marketing job, you can gain a lot of experience very quickly and the routes to managerial and responsible roles can be faster, and the rewards more immediate. This is a media job area in which an MBA is helpful, but not essential. A liberal arts degree or business major, with exposure to psychology, economics, advertising, and marketing can prove to be quite useful to you. In an agency or company, you can start at almost any job and gradually be exposed to other areas, ones which you may later find that you're attracted to more.

Advertising Statistical Clerk   Here you would compile and tabulate statistical records showing the cost of advertising, the volume of your client's advertising as compared with that of the competitors, the amount of the client's product that was sold after an advertisement as compared with the sales made before, and which ads were the most effective and which the least. The uses, benefits, and possibilities of statistical information are limitless.

Advertising or Media Clerk   If your business firm placed its own ads instead of using an agency, you would compile the advertising orders to submit to publishers or broadcasters. Or, if working in an agency, you would be sending out the advertising orders for the clients. As a clerk in an advertising medium such as radio or magazine, you would receive the ads from clients or agencies. The advertising or media clerk computes costs for an ad based on the size, date, position, number of times it's to be run, and the details involved in the ad's appearance. A responsibility of the job is to confirm that the advertisement was run and to insure proper billing. Other tasks are involved in verifying compliance with set specifications and this part of the job is interrelated with the duties of the Production Department.

Production Assistant   You receive the artwork and copy to be forwarded to the printer, broadcaster, mailing service, or film producer. This calls for follow-up on individuals who are behind in their schedule and not meeting deadlines. You learn to talk with typesetters, printers, film studios, recording specialists, artists, photographers, and designers. All the creative work of others goes nowhere if it doesn't pass through your hands—properly, on time, and with the right instructions.

Advertising Research Assistant   This is an entry-level job which many graduates may seek, and for good reason. It is an attainable and important way to learn the *realities* of the advertising business. Part of the task is to find out how your clients' products compare to the competition, which are best, and what are the salable features that can make your client's products seem better than others. You look for new ways to use products and how to sell them. You learn about the buying habits of customers and the effectiveness of the various advertisements used and their selling approaches. This work is related to that of a marketing researcher.

Marketing Trainee   Advertising and sales are heavily interlinked with marketing—a media business specialty relating to whether a product can be sold and where; who will buy it and at what price; the best way to design, package, and display it; what time of year to sell it, and to do so by using which displays, with what slogans or graphics; and whether sales will be stimulated by some kind of contest or coupon. This is an exciting and necessary part of business, but, admittedly, it can be

dull to a trainee who has to stand in a store with a counting de-
vice, clicking away the number of people who stop in front of
certain racks, pick up specific products, and decide to take or
leave them. And yet, this job is excellent training, and the information you collect, essential. From here, you can move up
to more responsible roles and decisions, with the next trainee
hired taking over your old duties.

Market Research Trainee   In this job, you go beyond the
role of advertising research assistant and often into realms beyond the marketing trainee. You become involved in researching and preparing reports on consumer preferences, their
habits, population trends, and on the sales growth of your company's products as compared to those of the competitors. You
use outside sources where appropriate, and being of an inquisi-
tive mind, you are actually a reporter. You will probably find
more independence and flexibility in doing your research in this
capacity, than in that of many others. A liberal arts degree is
helpful here and like the marketing trainee, will be aided by
having studied business, psychology, economics, statistics, and
computer operation.

Account Executive   In an advertising agency, an account
executive is not only the salesperson handling one or more clients on a personal basis, but is the liaison between a wide range
of working relationships that contribute to the selling function
as well. You work on plans catering to the client's marketing
and advertising needs, and coordinate the work between the
agency and the media to execute these plans and satisfy the client. Duties call for conferences with clients to suggest and/or
work within set budgets and objectives. The client with products or services to sell, looks to you and your agency as the
source of professional recommendations in selecting the appropriate media that will reach the desired customer market. You
must confer with agency artists, copywriters, photographers,
and other media-production specialists, and when needed, work
with outside sources.

As account executive, yours is a coordinating job—to bring
together the work of people engaged in marketing research,

copy writing, art preparation, media space and time buying, and many others, while as an individual, you must get involved in client activities, such as sales conventions. In short, you make sure all jobs are done and done well, fulfilling advertising and marketing needs and keeping your client from seeking another agency.

Advertising Sales   In advertising sales work, you are in a split-level role. With a newspaper or magazine, you might better be known as a publisher's representative; with a radio or television broadcaster, a time salesperson. You represent the advertising medium, trying to get advertising agencies or companies to use your facilities for running their ads. Often you have to help customers create their ads; other times you just receive and run what is produced by the companies or their agencies. Typically, this type of selling is on commission, with your earnings spread over a pay schedule, so to tide you over the slack sales periods in the year.

As a media representative, you may well find this a rewarding job both in terms of money and satisfaction. It can give you contacts that are useful in helping yourself and your employer. As with other sales jobs (beyond the routine type of clerical sales), this can be a profitable involvement if you have a good medium to sell and the initiative, self-motivation, and personality that attracts confidence and sales.

BROADCASTING

There are almost 150,000 full-time and 35,000 part-time workers in radio and television, plus several thousand freelance workers or independent contract personnel such as performers, musicians, artists, writers, and other specialists. Independent producers involved in the preparation of filmed or taped programs and commercials, plus radio-material firms, account for many jobs, too. Nearly half the jobs are professional or technical, such as announcers, newspersons, writers, and technicians. Although television accounts for slightly over ten per cent of the broadcasting stations, they provide more than forty per cent of the broadcast jobs. Here are some of the jobs involved, a number at entry level, others which utilize experience on school or public-service stations, and a few that require experience, but have responsibilities which even a beginner may be assigned to. To make a good impression and open doors in broadcasting, willingness, education, and personality are keys not to be forgotten.

Announcer   Both in radio and television the opportunities can be good, *if you have the talent and if you're willing to relocate.* About 30,000 jobs exist in this field, two-thirds in radio. A few specialty voice-recording firms and independent commercial producers use announcers as well but most of the starting jobs are in small stations. *It is here that you get experience,* and that experience is what will enable you to move on to other stations in larger communities. The average station employs four to six announcers, the bigger stations, more.

"I find that the main interest of young people who desire a career in broadcasting is as an announcer, DJ, or some kind of on-the-air personality," says Bob Silverman, head of a New York based broadcast barter advertising agency. "Unfortunately, the competition is so stiff that most kids don't make it here. And even when they do break in in this particular spot, they are often very disappointed with the pay. It's much lower than in sales."

In a small station, expect to work odd hours and at low starting pay. Here, as in large stations, you'll need a good speaking voice, the ability to ad-lib, good command of language, and to possess a sense of dramatism in your voice and presentation, in order to hold your audience. Small station duties are varied and you'll probably get a chance to sample them all. You could be assigned to broadcast sports, read commercials, deliver the news, do station-break announcements, forecast the weather, tell the time, play music, or even help operate the control board —anything and everything to keep the station on the air.

Knowing or becoming familiar with specialized areas such as sports or an area of music, will help you develop salable talents that can affect your position and income right from the start or off in the future. But on the other hand, many small stations announcers not only speak, but do their own writing, operate the control board, and even do sales work in addition. Being lightly staffed, the more things you do and the more things you are willing to pitch in on, the more valuable you become to the station.

Traffic Manager   This is the person who commands the minute-by-minute scheduling of programs and advertisements. The job requires good organizational skills and solid knowledge of the station's "on-air personality." This is frequently an additional duty for someone on a small station staff.

Continuity Director and Writer   This job requires delivering finished program and commercial scripts to the announcers, ones that maintain both the style of the individual announcer and the programming format established by the management.

Newswriter   Besides selecting news items and writing the script, the newswriter and newscaster, at a small station, are frequently one and the same.

Script Reader   This is related to a combination of duties: editor, lawyer, public representative. You read stories or scripts, review films or taped material prior to broadcast, to detect and delete undesirable material based on Federal Communications Commission (FCC) rules, and keep in alignment with management policies in regard to vulgar, immoral, libelous, false, biased, or misleading statements. Part of the duty can be recommending or performing editorial revisions. Often this job calls for discussions with sales and advertising agency personnel about discontinuing or revising commercials.

Film/Video Tape Editor   Almost all commercial television programming is recorded either on video tape or film. Live shows are videotaped for record purposes, parts of which may be extracted for replay at other times. Other shows are prerecorded for future broadcasts. Editors cut and splice all film and video tape for air presentation. They screen all films received by the station, whether it's from the staff or outside sources.

They cue all commercials, films, and tapes waiting to go on the air. They also edit locally produced films.

Film/Video Tape Librarian　*A film librarian is often needed at a station to catalog and maintain the files of tape and film used, know where to find needed segments, and how to get them fast in order to meet transmission deadlines.

Studio Operations　A variety of tasks need to be filled in an operating studio. For example, at a radio station the sound effects technician must simulate a variety of sounds—be it gunfire, or walking in the snow—and at a television station, a scenic designer plans and designs all studio settings and backgrounds. The point to remember about working in a studio is the more ready and capable and willing you are, the stronger your acceptance as a valuable staff member. You could be a floor manager, camera operator, make-up artist, audio technician, operate the teleprompter, supervise the studio's arrangement, or just type up program credits—there are many jobs to be done in the studio and how many people are hired to do them depends on the station's size and level of sophistication in programming.

DIRECTOR　Individual programs, or series, are planned and supervised by the director. This person is responsible for coordinating the show, selecting the artists and studio personnel, scheduling and conducting rehearsals, and directing the show during actual performance. Associated tasks include working with others in all details, distribution of scripts and making script changes. Assistants, in television, arrange for props, makeup, artwork, film slides, lighting, camera angles, camera selection, timing, cue cards, and cues to guide performers in movement and action.

PROGRAM DIRECTOR　Here is the person responsible for the overall programming schedule. Some programs are created locally, some are bought on a syndication basis, while others are brought in from network sources. The procurement of program material, personnel, scripts, facilities, use of outside services, scheduling, and a wealth of other details are involved in the job. Here is a varied, highly responsible job, toward which you evolve gradually, after you've learned about the component parts of the station.

Now that you have a better understanding of what the fields are about and what some of these media jobs entail, it's time to take a serious look at yourself. Let's find out how you can do a better job in selling *yourself,* and getting a start in the career of your choice.

Chapter 3

GETTING STARTED: MEASURING UP TO THE CHALLENGE OF JOB-SEEKING

SELF-EXPLORATION

Get what you want, and hope you want what you get. That's easier said than done. What you want can depend on your natural abilities, temperament, previous experiences, and advice received—not counting the opportunities, contacts, and breaks of many kinds. Give yourself a chance to improve your choices by reviewing what you know about yourself. By taking the time to appraise yourself carefully, you should be several steps nearer to the goals likely to satisfy you.

"If there's one thing that drives me crazy, it's talking to applicants who aren't sure what they want to do," says one disgruntled personnel director. "And even worse, half the time they haven't even figured out what their personal assets are, and how they can make a contribution to the company."

This chapter is to help you make such an analysis. Upon study, you'll find some areas which you enjoy or in which you are likely to respond well. Take note of them and start making a list. You should also make a list of the things you'd rather avoid, or which turn you off. In making decisions, everything you note about yourself counts.

WHAT DO YOU LIKE TO DO?

Do you have an inner drive which keeps you in hot pursuit of a task? You'd better know before you maneuver yourself into an inappropriate project by saying you want it, and then soon regret it. As an example, suppose you like to write. You already have education, training, and some experience, so you decide to write a book. Would your patience last for ten years on one book? That's a lot of time, effort, and constant plugging. Maybe you shouldn't tackle such a job. Yet, some people can and do attempt it. Fortunately, Margaret Mitchell was such a person. She was a reporter and feature writer for the *Atlanta Journal,* at which point an ankle injury caused her to give up reporting. She began the novel which ten years later was published under the title *Gone With the Wind.* It is wonderful when public and financial recognition follow, and while it doesn't always happen, in Mitchell's case she received the Pulitzer Prize for fiction the following year. Sales of her book sometimes hit 50,000 copies a day. The first year, 1.5 million copies were sold. Over 10 million copies have been printed, and the book has been translated into more than thirty languages. But then again, it *did* take ten years to write.

In analyzing yourself, it is appropriate to explore your interests. Do you have preference for working with *people, ideas,* or *things?* Certainly the areas overlap in jobs, but most positions are oriented to, or based primarily on your use of one of these three categories. Printing and broadcasting technicians mainly work with *things.* Writers and artists work with *ideas.* Secretaries, sales people, editors, and public relations representatives deal primarily with *people.* All of these roles, to a certain extent, involve people, ideas and things, but certain types of work would probably suit you best.

TRAITS TO CONSIDER

Grades, surprisingly, are low on the list of factors considered by potential employers. These media firms stress *personality,* the *willingness to learn,* and the *ability to fit into the company atmosphere* well. Executives seek well-rounded individuals who can communicate effectively and who have the basic education needed behind them. Once accepted, the company usually allows time for adjustment in getting accustomed to the organization and the job. The firm knows you will learn more as you proceed. The fact that you are agreeable and enthusiastic about any training program necessary, whether formal or informal, is important to the person hiring you. Sensing your drive and self-motivation can also be an important factor in getting hired. And on the job, by graciously accepting advice and asking about things you don't know, you usually can bring out assistance and help from knowledgeable coworkers who will get pleasure out of sharing their experience. All of these elements can help move you in surprising ways toward career goals and the day-to-day satisfactions that can accompany your progress. A former director of a large university's placement service has found that "responsibility and ability to follow through on an assigned task," is one of the major criteria employers apply when taking on new staff members. As said before, having top grades is usually lower down in the employer's list of desired qualities than some other things being considered—but, of course, it never hurts to have them. Here are eight common considerations by employers:

1. Character traits
2. Appearance and mode of traits
3. Speech and modes of self-expression
4. Manners
5. Degrees of self-confidence
6. Reliability
7. Control of temper and temperament
8. Ability to get along with others

"Too many young people have a chip on their shoulder when they go looking for jobs, and whether they know it or not, it shows," says Bob Silverman. "Attitude is very important."

"Dress is very important," says Jack Stern, President of his own New York art studio. "Even though we tend to dress casually once we have the job, I still look for someone who goes looking for a job in a suit. Someone who is neat in appearance. If they are sloppy, I tend to think that that is how their work is likely to be, too."

"Self-confidence is essential to growing into the job," states Jeffrey Feinman, President of Ventura Associates. "This is a crazy business with so much going on that some days it's almost impossible to keep up. If the staff doesn't have the confidence to speak up, ask questions, generate solutions to ideas, then they're going to be a drag to the business in the long run."

So in applying for a job, you would be standing in your own way if you let part of your background, grades, or lack of academic specialization in a particular subject slow you down in your efforts. For some jobs, additional specific training in a technical school may be helpful or even required. And do it, if necessary, but make sure to inquire ahead of time about the need for it before enrolling. Your potential employer may want to teach you on the job. Or, you may want to say you are willing to take job-related courses on your own time, which would satisfy the interviewer. Your attitude and willingness to study are frequently just as important as going on to another school for specialized training.

Some jobs are made for dominant, assertive people. They like to make decisions and like telling others what to do. If you enjoy giving orders and can become qualified at giving them, you've found a route toward becoming a manager. Yet there are ways of giving orders that get other people up-tight and thus disrupt the flow of the organization—the true leaders inspire their associates to give their all, and most enthusiastically at that.

Some jobs are for people who are happiest when their duties are spelled out for them. They like to follow instructions and do their best under competent supervision. Is this for you? Even if you are timid about making suggestions, embarrassed or apologetic about giving orders, you can do an excellent job as a specialist in your own area. Then why be miserable seeking a role as a supervisor? *Be good at what you're good at.*

Think about all of the hobbies that you have enjoyed and the activities that give you pleasure. Which elements in those involvements suit you the best? Is it physical action, meeting people, competition, the gathering of intriguing objects, seeing the results of your creativity, being inspired by new ideas or wanting to do something with them? All of these inclinations represent natural traits or orientations. *Don't ignore them in your search for a satisfying career.*

Personnel managers often feel that what you did in the past

indicates what you will do in the future. But conclusions about these portions of your past can fall by the wayside to a summary of your attitudes, skills, preferences, enthusiasm, responses, and relationships with other people, and the ability to stick to a task until finished—rather than giving the impression of giving up or continually seeking changes.

Ask yourself some pointed questions about the kind of contributions you can make to a potential employer. But keep in mind that, basically, you have little or no experience and therefore, initially, it will probably cost your employer money to hire you.

"The media fields attract lots and lots of hotshot young talent," says Richard Sachinis, President of The Graphic Experience, a New York multimedia agency, "but what they don't understand is that I will lose money on them for a year before they start to become productive. So even though a kid is hardworking and talented, companies just can't afford to pay them the kind of money they'd like to get. If kids want to get into any of the media professions, they'd better understand, right up front, that a low, low starting salary is part of the way the game works. If they go in thinking they can get big bucks, they're just wasting everybody's time."

During your working life, you will spend at least one-third of every working day on the job. If you want your career to be satisfying, you need to find one that is enjoyable, so that you look forward to the tasks in which you are involved. In your selection of a company or job, you *must* consider the number of hours you are willing to work, regularity or irregularity of those working hours, the commuting distance from your home, possibilities for advancement, use of your inner drive and wishes, opportunities to learn skills that will satisfy both you and others, the type of people you will be working with, and the potentials of job security. In addition, you must decide the kind of rewards and benefits you want, and how much money you'll need to make to afford the material things that can make your overall life more satisfying.

A sense of pride and fulfillment can keep you happy in a job; a lack of it will pressure you into contemplating changes. Company managers are aware of this and good ones will work hard to provide an atmosphere that keeps the employees happy and producing results that pay back (and hopefully surpass) the amount of time and money it took to hire and train them.

Do You Want to Work in a Small or Large Organization?

Are you a big-company person, or would you work more effectively in a smaller, less structured organization? There are good reasons for either choice from the start, or for switching later in your career from one to the other.

By starting with a small corporation, you are more likely to be exposed to the business as a whole and will be able more readily to understand *how* that particular business works. But many people don't like the idea of working in a small organization. Conversely, large corporations provide you with the experience you couldn't get elsewhere of how a "big business" operates. But many people don't like the anonymity that can occur in big organizations. If you're not sure which you want, talk with people who are working at both kinds of corporations to get a feel for which appeals to you the most. Naturally, you'll never really know until you've worked for a large or a small company, but even without specific experience, you should have an idea of the structure you'd be most happy working within. You may find it helpful to examine the types of social interactions in which you are most happy and comfortable.

Many, many high-level jobs are held by people who originally started with tiny companies, or in relatively small towns. Here is where you can get a variety of experience that is almost impossible to gain in a large, intricately structured organization. For example, occasionally being switched from a writing task to dealing with an advertiser will broaden your exposure. When a key person is out sick or on vacation, somebody has to attend to essential duties, and in a small office it may well be you.

If you are the only one available in a media office, you may suddenly find yourself ordering printing, talking to members of the press, handling problems of a customer, pursuing an order through the production stages, contacting outside suppliers, or having to give answers in the absence of a salesperson. Any one of these experiences can open up an entirely new area of interest and possibility for you.

Also, one of these experiences might be the wedge exposing a broader knowledge and the genuine ability to say, "Yes, I've done it before," when a good opportunity comes along. It is highly unlikely that you would get an editing or reporting job on a big-city newspaper without having previous on-the-job training—and where are you going to get it? School newspaper jobs usually don't count, but capability in handling a variety of assignments at a small newspaper *does,* and this is where to get the prestige and apprenticeship that enables you to move up when the time comes. In effect, get a good education and be paid to receive it!

"In a small operation, you are in the spotlight," says Richard Sachinis of The Graphic Experience, who began his career at a large corporation, "and everything you do is not only very important, but it's noticed, too. In a large company, you've got many more people to help you and you can break the job into components. If you've got problems, there are a lot of people you can go to for help. In a small company, the same job is tougher, because you are part of the front line troops. There's a lot more pressure, but if you can survive it all, then you're the star. You're the one who got the job done and it's you who gets the credit. If you work well under pressure, if you're dedicated to getting the job done—and getting it done right—then you'd probably shine in a small company. But if pressure is hard for you, and you can't handle it, look for a lower-key job. Because sooner or later it's going to get to you, you'll be bitter and frustrated. And believe me, that's no way to work."

IMMEDIATE AIMS

In a larger company, let's suppose the Personnel Director has a request for a secretary or typist. And let's suppose you want to be an editor, producer, account executive, or some other title professional. If you show too much ambition and imply you won't stay long as a secretary, then you won't get the job. Personnel has a job to fill, not your career wishes to humor. So know what to say, and what you will settle for at the moment, despite the goals you have set for yourself. You can be frank that you want to work yourself up after putting in sufficient time in the job that fulfills the company's immediate needs. Your educational record proves that you have ambition and capability, or you would not (and could not) have gone to college or taken up specialized training in the first place. Most companies don't want to take a risk on a newcomer in a more responsible job, until he or she has been observed in an entry-level one and inspires confidence in being ready and able to handle a more important position.

When seeking an entry-level job, be mentally attuned for whatever salary is offered. Time, opportunities, friendships, and job changes can alter that and sooner than the initial job-offer implies. Being on the scene is Step Number One.

When applying for a job, if you are good at typing, detailed work, handling complaints, talking on the phone, working with numbers, or anything which can be useful to the company, make sure to tell about it. Displaying enthusiasm and self-confidence go far, too. Emphasize all of your good points, so it seems to the person you're interviewing with that there are more and more reasons to hire you and very few for not doing so.

What Do You Want Out of a Job?

A fast track with plenty of opportunities despite tough competition and problems? Or do you want security and a low-pressured working situation? *Are Your Goals Feasible?* Do they suit your personality and traits, or should your goals be altered more realistically?

From the very onset of job hunting, you must do some exploring to see whether you are the right sort of person for the kind of job you are seeking. You may find that you'd be better off by moving in another direction. Just take the time to pick your *own* direction and then choose the speed at which you're willing to pursue your objectives.

FOCUSING IN ON YOUR GOALS

Finding the kind of work best suited for you may seem a hard task, but it can be done. You need to sift through your many capabilities, needs, likes, dislikes, and thoughts before making any choices.

RESEARCHING JOB TYPES

Before you make up your mind to apply for a job, or accept the first one that comes along, use the wealth of information available to you on library shelves and elsewhere. For instance, there is an overwhelming amount of material published by the U. S. Government about the job markets. Some of it is sold; much of it is free.

There are thousands of job types held by the 100-million people who work in the United States. All of them are listed in a directory issued by the U. S. Government Printing Office, entitled *Standard Occupational Classification Manual*. And to expand on the title listing in that book, there is a companion volume called *Dictionary of Occupational Titles*. Any type of position in publishing, advertising, public relations, radio, television, or film is described there, and the duties and skills related to each are briefly outlined. Read through these books— there are 20,000 different jobs described—and use them to expand your knowledge of occupational horizons.

For more assistance, the U. S. Department of Labor regularly publishes an updated edition of a large volume called *Occupational Outlook Handbook*. In it, you can find a great deal of information concerning 300 of the most frequently called for types of jobs or careers. A large number of them have a specific place within the media professions, or in a supporting aspect upon which media companies depend.

If you are having difficulty in finding out exactly what you want to do, but do know what natural abilities you have, try looking through the *Guide for Occupational Exploration* (also published by the U. S. Department of Labor). It tells you how and where your various capabilities can be used, and introduces a scope of industries which you may never have considered. Occupations are listed by interest, traits, and abilities, in order to help identify and explore possible areas of work for you.

Besides broadening your horizons in the kinds of jobs you can seek, there is another very important rationale behind reading these lengthy and somewhat tedious texts. If you are completely undecided about your career path, or have been rejected too many times in a specific field, these texts provide the specific information that allows you to approach the job market with a real sense of purpose that will lead, hopefully, to your first job in the profession of your choice.

For those of you still unsure about yourselves, make a list of all your personal characteristics. (This is often difficult to do by yourself, so don't hesitate to ask a person who knows you to help out.) Think of appealing occupations and the ways you could use your qualifications. Talking to friends, relatives, and people who know you is fine—*but don't stop there.* Use the U.S. government sources mentioned and search for career directions you may have overlooked. You can't wait for a job to be dangled in front of you like a $1,000 bill, you've got to go out knowledgeably and find it. Finally, once you've set your career goals, go out on interviews *prepared* and *enthusiastic* and thus improve your chances of getting that job you really want.

RESEARCHING A COMPANY'S IMAGE: WHAT THEY LOOK FOR

A student with an A average has just been interviewed for admission to an advertising agency as a trainee Account Executive. He specialized in marketing, has his Master's, was involved in a number of prestigious campus groups, and has good letters of recommendation. But the interviewer's report about him says: "Do not recommend hiring." Here are some of the reasons noted:

- He was nervous during the lengthy conversation. He could not relax despite my changing to familiar topics where he might be more at ease. He was unable to con-

verse or respond without lengthy, deliberate considerations. He had trouble replying to questions for which
he was not prepared.

- He had fixed mannerisms, or ones that intruded. He
  stared straight ahead, instead of looking me in the eye.
  His fingers kept tapping his knees or my desk constantly.

- Despite excellent grades, he changed his direction of
  studies in school several times. I am not certain he would
  stick to our A.E. job, or the training program, confirmed
  by his inability to summarize clearly what his career
  goals are.

- His résumé and application had obvious spelling mistakes, as well as grammatical errors, and these were slop-
  pily prepared. If he did this with business letters or presentations given to our clients, it would reflect negatively
  upon our company.

- His letters of recommendation were good, but not highly
  enthusiastic enough, based on many other letters I see. I
  have the suspicion that each person who wrote a letter of
  recommendation had some personal reservations, so that
  we are seeing a "powder puff" letter indicating there isn't
  too much solid substance about which to write.

Having high grades in school and a good record of involvement in clubs or sports doesn't necessarily get you a job. More
and more, personality, dress, mannerisms, ease in relating to
people, ability to deal with surprise questions, and other elements not taught in the classroom, have become the critical
points upon which the decision to hire someone is made.

"Personal appearance is very important," says Bob DeLay,
President of the Direct Mail/Marketing Association. "I look
for clean clothes, shined shoes and conservative dress. The reason I consider this to be important is that many times I will interview people who have what appear to be equal capabilities.
Then I have to look to other aspects of them. Did I like them?
How were they dressed? What kind of enthusiasm did they
show? Any of these characteristics can give a person a competitive edge over someone else. As far as dress is concerned, you

should dress like the kind of person you want to be. Show taste. Women should probably not wear slacks on an interview."

"If you want to be considered for a job with growth, then you've got to look the part," says an executive at a large corporation. "Dress not for the job you have, but for the one you want to have. When you look like an executive, you're a lot more likely to be noticed and considered for such a job. If you enter the field as a secretary, and if you dress like one (and it's easy to fall into that trap), then you are likely to limit yourself to being a secretary. And that's a sure way to stunt your career path."

"Many companies have a corporate *image*," says an Associate Editor at one of the major publishing houses. "And if you don't look the part, dress the part and act the part, then you're just never going to make it there."

It's true. Many large companies do have an image. In your job search, see if you can find out what that image is before you go on an interview. Obviously, you don't want to change yourself to fit the company, but sometimes it will give you a competitive edge if you know enough to stress certain things that will appeal to that particular company. If you can't get that information in advance, or find that the company doesn't seem to have a clear cut image, then play it safe—dress conservatively, act conservatively, and look for clues once you are there.

"I want people to have a positive attitude," says John Pahmer, Marketing Consultant. "By this I mean that there should be an attitude on their part to make a lot of money—for the company and for themselves. It evidences itself by what the person says, where that person goes, and what that person likes to do. I avoid people who say they like to stay home and read books.

"Also, there is a fine line in interviews which an applicant must be careful not to cross," John Pahmer continues, "I'm delighted when they are relaxed and casual, but I don't like it when they get cocky."

Executives look at far more than talent and high grades when it comes to making the final decision, so make sure you show that potential employer that *you do* offer more.

Finding Out What Jobs Are Available

To the rest of the world, you don't exist, until that time you let them know you're here.

To announce your presence, you have to publicize. Do it by personal appearance, writing, or through someone who'll speak in your behalf. Your application for a job is actually an advertisement to sell your own services. When you talk to others, write letters, and prepare a résumé, you are doing a public relations task in which you are your own client. Do a good job.

Let it be known that *you* are available, that you are ready, willing, and able to accept a job. Not any old job, but one with specific involvements that satisfy a lot of your career desires. Your desires include making use of your education, your capabilities, your previous experiences, your personal inclinations, your ambitions, and all of the other elements that have created the *you* that exists and wants to move ahead.

"If an applicant isn't sure what he wants, it's a real turn off," says the marketing director at a large packaged goods company. "I want them looking for a specific job. My role is to put them into a position, not be a counselor. That should be done before they ever get here."

In *saying* what you want, or asking for a specific type of job, through a conversation, letter, telephone call, or résumé, you are announcing your availability. To eventually get what you want, you must decide what you will initially settle for, and to do that, you must find out about as many job openings as you can so as to be able to compare the opportunities. And if the world isn't clamoring to offer you a job, start spreading the word! Consider some of the methods other people used to find their way into a job.

Relatives, Friends, Associates   "I am always much more receptive to an applicant who comes to me via a recommendation. It gives me a chance to check them out in more detail than I can as the result of a cold mailing," says Martin Cohn, Creative Supervisor for Ogilvy & Mather Direct Response, San Francisco Branch.

This is, of course, a starting point to make the most of. Even if your parent or friend is employed by a company that you have no interest in working for, remember that people may often hear of work that does interest you, places that are in need of capabilities such as yours, and where there are friends upon whom you might call. Be open to the variety of ways others can help you. Take the time to list all of the people you know or have met. Include school associates, acquaintances, people connected to the profession you might want to enter, such as neighbors, members of clubs you belong to, and groups to which your friends or relatives belong. With enough thinking, the list should be lengthy. Then take that list and let everyone on it know what you are looking for.

Newspaper and Trade Publication Ads   These are good sources for job availabilities, and can often offer insight about whatever job markets you're interested in. Start looking in your local publications, and those of nearby towns and cities. Then look at professional trade publications in the field for which you are trained or want to enter. Many of these periodicals can be found at libraries, or in the very offices you visit in your job-hunt. Their names are in *Ulrich's* list of periodicals, *Ayer's Directory,* or *Literary Market Place.* Nor should you overlook ads found in various sections of publications like the Sunday New York *Times,* or the *Wall Street Journal.*

Don't hesitate to respond to an ad, even if it has been a few days since the advertisement first appeared. Positions are seldom filled immediately. But, in general, keep in mind that a prompt reply is best. It's a subtle way of showing your enthusiasm and ability to act quickly. Make your letter of application tailor-made to fit the advertisement. Answer all questions and expand on what you think they're really looking for. Your letter is a cover-letter—a personal introduction to your résumé that is attached. Or you may choose to combine the main elements of your résumé into the body of a one-page letter. This kind of personal, yet time-saving touch for the potential employer, can make a difference in getting attention.

"When we advertise for an entry-level position in adver-

tising," says Risa Bell of Zimmermann Marketing, "we are
likely to get hundreds of replies. Therefore, as one of the scan-
ning techniques, I check to see if the applicant made the effort
to personalize the résumé and/or cover letter to the particular
job. If someone took the time to target a reply, that is a definite
help towards getting an interview."

If appropriate, use your imagination and talent in expression.
Instead of the routine "I wish to apply for your job . . ." type
of letter, think about what else you could do with writing and
layout to grab their attention and create the desire to invite you
in for an interview. Most letters have about three to five sec-
onds to either get attention, or go on their way to a dead-end
file. Can your opening words and attention-getter beat the
odds? *Work at it.* (See Chapter 4 The Résumé, for more details.)

Mailing Out Résumés   In desperation or inspiration, somewhere along the line you may be inclined to send out dozens or
even hundreds of résumés. Expect less than three invitations
for an interview out of every hundred résumés sent out—*even if
you are in a marketable field.* Your chances are even less if
your field is flooded with job-seeking applicants having similar
education or training. This is often the case in media and poses
problems for many liberal arts students and graduates. There
aren't many calls for art history majors, specialists in medieval
history, or even graduates in English literature. So you must approach the reality of media job-searching with a variety of tac-
tics.

"So many people who want to get into the media fields go
about looking for jobs in such a manner that they are bound to
quickly get discouraged," says Annette Swanstrom, Executive
Vice-President for Prescott Lists, a New York media agency.
"Sending out résumés 'cold' can be one of the worst ways because you get so few responses. That's not to say you shouldn't
do it, because I know people who have gotten jobs that way.
But don't limit yourself to that aspect of the job hunt. There
are many more ways, and you've got to use them all."

As we have said before (and will say again), emphasize your

special talents, achievements, capabilities, and personal qualities welcomed by most employers such as reliability, drive to finish a task, self-motivation, and a pleasant telephone voice. Abilities like typing or operating a computer terminal deserve promotion as well.

"Nowadays, typing can be a real key to getting a job," Annette Swanstrom continues. "For me, I do my best thinking at the typewriter. Also, there are many times it's extremely important to get something out *immediately,* and if I have to wait for the secretarial pool, it can ruin the whole impact of what I'm trying to do. Young people looking for jobs can stress their typing ability from two points. One, it is a marketable skill which could get them in the door. And two, even if they are being hired at a level above secretary, it can help them in assisting on the job. From what I can see today, typing is an almost indispensable skill at the entry level."

Whatever the mailing piece you are sending, type it professionally and *address it to the name and title of the person you want to read it.* Every profession has directories that list people by name and title but if you lack this, a telephone call to the company's switchboard operator can produce the name of that person you want to receive your letter. Start with higher-ranking titles, rather than low ones. Résumés almost never get passed upward, but can easily be buck-slipped to the right person in a position to call you. Address your envelopes to people in jobs related to the area where you want to work, not just to "President, XYZ Company."

Employment Agencies   While some companies do not use employment agencies, feeling they can do just as well on their own, many do. You would do well to do a little research and find out what the agency's reputation is in industry circles. Some agencies are good; others can be mass-market résumé-mailers that flood employers with applicant summaries, hoping that at least one of the people described will be invited to interview. There are agencies who specialize in certain fields of media work, such as publishing or radio and television. And there are a few agencies who have worked closely with their clients and over a period of time have established a professional relationship that gives them an access to personnel and management departments that nobody else can match. These agencies know what is going on in the organization and in the industry as a whole. In conversations with people you meet, like a personnel manager, ask them to suggest the name of an agency they respect and a person in it they think is worth seeing. However, if you use an agency, unless you've got some really special qualifications, be prepared for the fact that you'll probably need to know how to type.

Look at the advertisements in periodicals to see which agencies specialize in the areas you are interested in. You might start there, even though a specific job you want has not been advertised. By doing this, the agency may call you about a job opening before they run an advertisement. Also, don't judge an agency by the size of its ads.

An agency will probably request your résumé and then prepare a different, one-page version, that fits the agency style. Ask to see what is prepared and be sure that your important qualifications and career-objectives have not been left out. In terms of fees, most agencies do not charge professional personnel for their services, but receive a commission from the employer that hires their client. If you do not want to pay a fee, make sure to ask what the agency's policy is before signing any forms.

Government Employment Services   A lot of government money and work has gone into establishing a national employment network of about 2,500 offices, complete with computer networks, guidance personnel, sales efforts, and job-training connections. Originally, the purpose of this service was to get people off the unemployment and welfare rolls, but now its function far surpasses that goal. Many levels of jobs are handled, including administrative, sales, management, and technical positions. The computer and publication facilities link local, state, and national needs, so if you are seeking a job in another state, the service can help. A self-service file, listing jobs in many types of work, is available to you for inspecting and selecting openings for which you wish to apply.

It can be well worth it to get your name into the files of the government's employment service data bank. You will be interviewed to note your qualifications, education, experience, and preferences. Just as with other job applications, the advance thinking that has gone into your résumé and the self-analysis you have done about your capabilities can improve the quality of the listing you leave in their hands.

To find the location of the nearest government employment-service office, look in the telephone directory under the name of your state. Within that heading should be a subheading such as Labor Department or Employment Services. "Job Service Office" or "State Employment Service" are the customary titles you are looking for. It is at these offices, too, that you can find out about federal, state, and local government jobs, ones which are not usually listed elsewhere.

Government employees and their dependents account for about one-eighth of the nation's population, while another ten per cent of private employment exists because of government spending. So don't ignore this job-hunting ground when trying to get a start in your career.

School Placement Offices   Many school job counselors and alumni offices get involved in attempting to match alumni or students to jobs. Even if they don't have a job for you or specific names, their advice can be helpful. Companies or individuals they recommend could put you on the road toward opportunities you might not have encountered otherwise.

Executive-Search Firms   These companies sound impressive when you read their advertisements in certain trade or large-city newspapers. They get paid for their time, and are on specific assignments, to find people who can fill high-level or specialty positions. Usually you have to be in an upper bracket to make it worth their while to work with you. So for the entry-level or fairly low-experience rung, this is probably not a good job-seeking source for you. If a firm calls itself executive-search and charges a fee, then it probably is really an employment agency or job-counseling service.

Job Counselors   If a firm offers job-counseling, it usually is not in the employment business, though it may have behind-the-scenes affiliations with executive-search firms or employment agencies. Job-finding is possible here, but not guaranteed. For a considerable fee, paid by you, analysis and consultation is done on your education, background, and experience. Detailed psychological tests are given to find out what fields your inclinations lie toward. Fees are typically costly and your own self-analysis may take you just as far in finding out what job areas appeal to you. Usually there is an introductory discussion about their services at no charge, so if you are curious, you may want to inquire.

Professional Societies   Possibly you belong to a professional society, or are eligible to join one. If the group has a placement service, inquire about the procedure for receiving help in your job-hunt. The society may periodically sponsor employment related mailings, or be called upon by employers seeking people with the talent usually possessed by the members of such a group.

"Position Wanted" Ads   Results from advertising your availability are usually marginal. But, on the other hand, all you need is one good inquiry. Generally, these advertisements are only effective when there is a shortage of the kinds of skills and capabilities that you possess. However, you never know, it may be worth placing an ad.

Temporary Jobs   Consider agencies that provide assistants to companies for a certain period of time. If you are unable to get practical experience elsewhere, a temporary job can give you the ground to build on. At least you would be in the working environment of your preferred career area, *where you can see and be seen,* and possibly be invited to join the regular staff.

Temporary jobs can last from a day to a week to a number of months, and sometimes even longer. Companies use temporary help to deal with peak work-load periods instead of hiring full-time staff members and then later having to terminate their employment in a slow period. Temporary jobs open up a world of possibilities for people who want or need to work at irregular hours or only on certain days.

Pay scales can be higher than those of the regular employees at the same company, but without the benefits (life or medical insurance, or a pension). You are the employee of the agency that sends you on assignment, but keep in mind that the temporary job can often turn into permanent position with the firm you are assigned to. At the very least, being a "temp" will keep your skills sharp, increase your knowledge, give you income, and expose you to opportunities and contacts that may come to be quite useful in starting your career.

Freelance   "Doing freelance work can be a wonderful way to work yourself into a job. I did it myself in the early stages of my career. Never be reluctant to take on freelance assignments," RoseMarie Brooks of *Sport* magazine continues. "It's a good way to keep learning and make lots of contacts that can help later on." Many writers start by freelancing and sometimes prefer to continue, or they maintain it as a sideline. Generally, it's advisable not to depend on making a living by doing freelance work, since a lot of it is done on speculation, or by people who already have a job. Sources such as those listed in *Writer's Market* (published annually), give lengthy descriptions of the demand and rates of payment. Persistence, perception, and self-motivation are essential here, in addition to turning out good material.

In other occupations, freelance or independent agents can be found as well. A typical example is the actor or model appearing in a commercial, or a training, educational, or special-purpose film. Producers turn to agents who represent a selection of likely and available talent. Similarly, many radio scripts, television plots, and projects for business organizations come from freelancers.

The independence of being a freelancer is either the blessing or curse of many artists. And while working as an independent agent or freelancer is not being examined in this book, it is a way of marking time until you've found a full-time job of your choice.

A Note on Starting Your Own Business   Someday this may be appropriate, but is it now? A successful business calls for having the right product and services at the right time and the right employees, financing, entrepreneurial drive, contacts, and willingness to take risks. Otherwise, it is safer and more practical to work for someone else. *Fortune* magazine examined this subject at one time and came up with the same conclusion. So if you have noticed that this book sticks to getting hired by someone, then you should know that it does so for good reason. *Learn at others' expense.* Use their facilities, training, and experience to boost you on the ladder of success. The idea of your own business shouldn't be put out of your mind indefinitely, but *don't* make it your first move.

ARMING YOURSELF FOR THE JOB HUNT

Assume that you will need six months, at least, to get located in a media job. This should give you the mental and emotional stamina to keep plugging, and even if you've already put in that much time, set another six-month goal for yourself and begin again right now. Chances are you'll utilize a lot more resources, more efficiently, the second time around.

KEEPING A NOTEBOOK

One very practical idea, suggested by a personnel director, is for you to keep notes. You can't possibly remember everything encountered in an intense, effective, job-search process, so here are a few ways you can record the bits and pieces of information that might tip the hand in your favor.

An Idea Page: Write any thoughts, suggestions or ideas you have received onto the Idea Page. Write down names of companies, jobs, people, or possible opportunities. If a few minutes of writing fills many lines, then more are likely to occur later. Committing your ideas to paper can pull you out of a hole and spark your forward-motion.

Don't cross off things you have tried before, and don't let competition scare you off. Renew your determination with the Idea Page, increase your efforts and make effective pursuit pay off.

Contacts to Make: Prepare a work sheet on ruled paper and make columns for such information as name of company, location, person to contact, source of idea, date to contact, and comments. If a follow-up visit or phone-call is needed, note when to make it and in such a way that it won't be forgotten.

Diary of Contacts: Keep a record of who you have seen, when, and what was said. Some people will be worth approaching again, or you may have to refer back to the list for another reason. The point is, why put a strain on your memory when a good diary lists everything worth recalling? Your diary sheet includes name of company, location, date of contact or interview, name of interviewer(s), results and comments. Make notes of any papers you showed or left there.

Follow Up on Your Notes: A collection of paperwork is useless if you ignore the ideas, invitations, job-leads, and other information that is contained in them.

Now that you have an idea of the many ways you can begin to look for a job, and are aware of some specific things you can do to prepare for that interview, it's time to start thinking aggressively.

PSYCHING UP

The purpose of your application for a job, through whatever source, is to get you an interview. That is where the payoff is. In an application of *any* sort, your goal is always the same: to sell yourself as the person capable of filling the employer's needs. But selling is a two-way process. The employer has questions to ask, and that is where the interviewing process comes in. The techniques of interviewing are quite varied, so you must become well versed in what to say and how to act in different situations. There will be more on interviews later.

As we have said before, looking for, and finding, a job is a six-month process, on the average. It is natural, therefore, that rejections will be part of that process. Being continually rejected is a common experience and almost everyone has gone through it, so don't count on being an exception. The fields of media work are crowded with more applicants than the job market can possibly absorb. You must remember that it's your imagination, contacts, efforts, personal appearances, telephone calls, experience from interviews and your total plan of attack that, somewhere along the line, is going to give you that desired and necessary edge over the others.

Sure you get depressed after being rejected. It hurts. This is just as true, if not more so, when you have gone through several interviews for a specific job, only to be turned down in the final selection. The important thing is to recognize when your self-esteem is sinking and to remember that with the next success, *you'll bounce back*. If you lose your drive, confidence, or start building self-doubts, you will be hurting yourself and this is the reason for planning a long-range job-search program. Expect rejections, and when they occur, rise above them.

"Make up your mind that it's not going to be easy," says Thomas Moore, President, Tomorrow Entertainment, Inc. "It takes time. That's the way it is. Don't think that the first call is going to result in a job. And don't be frightened by rejection.

"Look at every interview as a chance to better you and your technique, rather than a rejection. In fact, rehearse the interview before you go in, and afterwards, speak to someone knowledgeable on the subject and explain to them about the interview, and find out ways that you can improve your interviewing technique. In fact, if you've been able to develop some kind of rapport with the person who interviewed you, there's certainly nothing wrong with asking the interviewer for advice on how you can interview better."

Latch onto words of encouragement and good receptions that you *do* get, and use them as fuel for motivation. After all, you would not have gotten those responses if you didn't merit attention. For example, a once struggling author tried to sell a book which, and it's on record, was rejected by fifty (fifty!)

publishers. All of them sent the book back with a rejection letter, varying from *no,* to cordial ones admiring the work and explaining why they couldn't sign it up. It was on the fifty-first try that an editor said "I like it . . . and can you write two more books, in the same style, for a series?" Within the next two years, four more books were contracted with the author.

Don't give up.

Chapter 4

THE RÉSUMÉ

WHAT IT IS

A résumé is a summary, a blueprint of you—your education, background, goals and related experience—and it is a basic, vital, written step in an effective job search.

Many people think that you must have solid work experience in order to have a good résumé, but that's not necessarily true. Jobs and background can't guarantee a good résumé, just as superior products can't guarantee a good salesperson. Whether you've worked part time during summers, or never had a job, you still can create a résumé that will get you a job.

WHY IT IS SO IMPORTANT TO HAVE A GOOD ONE

Why is a good résumé so important? Your résumé is usually the first impression that prospective employers will have of you, and since you want to continue that into second and third meetings, you should make it good. Résumés are the conventional form of introduction to prospective employers and are used to screen applicants. Because of this, you need to state quickly, concisely, and effectively why they should want to find out more about you and grant an interview. You may be competing with hundreds of other applicants for a prospective employer's attention, so you've got to *make sure your résumé works quickly and aggressively to sell you and your capabilities.*

"Because I receive so many résumés," says one personnel director at a major network, "I've got to do a lot of prescreening. I go a lot on first impressions. Is the envelope typed? Is there a cover letter? Is the résumé error-free?"

A good résumé describes your past experience, background, and future goals, and often on just a single sheet of paper. But a good résumé doesn't only tell what you've done, it also *implies what more you can do*. Though it is not easy to come up with a winning résumé right away, if you put time, creative thought, and carefully chosen words into it, your résumé can pay off in an interview for you, rather than another person.

When applying for an entry-level position in a media profession, you're going to be up against some stiff competition. It's not uncommon for an entry-level opening in broadcasting, publishing, or advertising to attract as many as 1,000 applicants for the job! Though that number may seem overwhelming (and more than a bit discouraging, too), keep in mind that most of the applicants' résumés will be, in one way or another, unacceptable by professional standards.

"In the course of a year, hundreds of résumés cross my desk," says Tim Sharpe, General Manager of McCann-Erickson Direct Response, a division of the McCann-Erickson advertising agency. "Most of them are so poorly executed that there is no incentive for me to speak with these candidates." Indeed, most executives say that the majority of résumés they've seen—whether from people with advanced academic degrees, people who have had twenty years of business experience, or people who have never held more than a part-time job—are dull, poorly organized, too wordy, not informative enough, or in some way, just not very appealing.

Even if you're about to get your Bachelor's degree or have never held a paying job before, just putting time and thought into the construction of your résumé can give you the competitive edge over hundreds of other applicants. In fact, with a great, well thought out résumé, you can actually beat someone else, with better qualifications, out of an interview.

HOW TO MAKE YOURS STAND OUT

In writing your résumé, you must keep one thing in mind: *business runs on profits*. Don't waste anyone's time with superfluous information or a three-page résumé when one page will do. Show your prospective employer, right from the start, that you are interested in helping the company make money.

Again, though it may seem repetitious, it cannot be stressed enough that *the main aim of business is to make a profit,* and in business, time is money. *Don't waste any business person's time by sending a résumé that is longer or wordier than need be. Keep it short and to the point.* If you're just getting out of college, or have little work experience, you certainly should be able to fit your main selling points on one sheet of paper. (You shouldn't need more than a one-page résumé until you are at least five years into your career.)

Understandably, it seems quite difficult to boil down all that you are—all those years of living and experiencing—into a couple of tight paragraphs that will represent and sell you in the job marketplace. *But that is exactly what you must do.* This requires writing everything out and then deciding (perhaps with the help of a trusted, objective friend or relative) what your selling points are. Then you must keep combining, rewording, and cutting until you come up with a few concise, well-worded, lucid paragraphs.

To present your past experience to a potential employer in the most profitable light, use creative insight. What you've got to do is look at your past experience and ask yourself, "How could my background be profitable to a business?" You've got to take your activities and assets out of their original context and transform them with a new eye cast toward profits—making money, saving money, saving time, increasing organization—so that you or your prospective employer can place a value on what you've done.

The following example shows how even a volunteer's experience can be presented as profit-oriented capabilities in business:

Suppose that you worked for three years during college as a volunteer counselor at a crisis hotline center. This experience shows that you have worked on an essential project, are able to work well under pressure, keep a level head in an emergency situation, have worked effectively within an organization and know how the structure of one functions, shown responsibility and loyalty to your job and that you possess a genuine sensitivity and caring for others.

Try to be objective as you translate your activities and accomplishments from their original context into that of profits. Though it may be easy to think, "Oh, that wasn't important," when looking at something you did, stop and reconsider—you may be passing over the most revealing and profit-oriented aspect of your background. Be creative, objective, and above all, *confident* when you assess your accomplishments. By doing that, a "something I just did," may well turn into a "something that means profits for you" on your résumé.

THE NEED FOR MORE THAN ONE

Once you have done your homework and are well versed in the variety of entry-level positions within the media professions, you will see, happily, that you have many choices. And any one of them could start you on the ladder of success in your dream career.

If you are proficient in many areas, have a lot of interests, and think you could be happy in any one of a variety of fields, then you would do best by writing more than one résumé, each presenting a different set of career goals. It is possible to put all of your different objectives and interests into one résumé, but it is most advisable that you concentrate only on one or two major selling points in any résumé and here's why: If you include a number of goals within the same résumé, it becomes obvious that you don't know exactly what you want to do and, generally, this registers poorly with executives. You are much better off in constructing résumés to meet specific objectives. Don't be scared off by the idea of writing two, three, or even four, since they require only a little more work than one résumé demands. Rather than totally rewriting each résumé, all you need do is construct a single general résumé and use it as a building block for the others.

With each résumé, you need to slant your presentation. In every case, you should change your career objective and tailor-fit your background (education, activities, and experience) to each version. For instance, suppose you've received your BA in English with a minor in Broadcasting, and you're interested in either going into book publishing or film production. In altering your general résumé to fit publishing, you should first state your career objectives in those terms. Then, secondly, you should identify those courses you took that relate to book publishing, such as those in literature and writing. But then when you gear your résumé to broadcasting, you should state in your career objectives that you want an entry-level position in broadcasting, eventually leading you to a career in film production. Then you should mention all of the courses you took that relate to broadcasting and film production. If you attempted to combine these two different career objectives into one résumé, the outcome would be confusing, to say the least. "When I receive a résumé with more than one career goal," says Malcolm Smith, Vice-President, Ventura Associates, "I figure that the person hasn't decided what he or she wants to do yet. I want people here who are sure of themselves."

In addition to slanting your education toward different areas, you should also isolate any pertaining work experience and highlight interests, extracurricular activities, and hobbies as they relate to your stated career goal. Again, even if you haven't had any "real" experience in a media field, if presented in the right light, your course work, interests, and hobbies will go a long way in convincing the prospective employer that you have the potential to help achieve the company's goals.

TRANSLATING YOUR EXPERIENCE INTO POTENTIAL

Even if you've never had a job before, you've undoubtedly had certain types of experience that are valuable to business. What constitutes experience? Involvement in college clubs, sports, class projects, extracurricular activities, or various hobbies—they can all provide the material for developing experience and potential. If you lack participation in these areas, then you might want to consider doing some volunteer work for experience. This is especially helpful if your volunteer efforts are somehow related to the field you are interested in pursuing.

"Today's more affluent young person has not necessarily had the need to find work before completing schooling," says Heidi Bermacher, Advertising and Sales Promotion Manager for Travel and Lodging division of the American Express Company. "If I see that volunteer work is included on a résumé, especially in the field, I am favorably impressed."

The following is a list of generalized capabilities and traits that, when translated into specific instances, can be very valuable to businesses:

CAPABILITIES

TRAITS

communicating	self-discipline	creativity
speaking	self-confidence	goal orientation
planning	discretion	congeniality
coordinating	manageability	independence
administrating	perseverence	analytical abilities
writing	sincerity	efficiency
evaluating	fairness	loyalty
analyzing	precision	decisiveness
setting priorities	adaptability	follow-through
educating	reliability	responsibility
selling	enthusiasm	motivation
organizing	dynamism	compatibility
editing	team-orientation	competence
people skills	objectivity	tact
budgeting	ability to take risks	ability to concentrate
supervising	detail orientation	ability to work under stress

Consider *all* of these capabilities and traits, and use them as a guide for exploring your background and developing your strong, frequently exhibited, positive selling points and characteristics. In addition, if your job experience is limited, or non-existent, these lists should lead you to discover what aspects of your experience are valuable to business. These aspects should be included in your résumé.

In putting together your résumé, *you've got to be descriptive*. Whether you had a paying job or were a member of an extracurricular club, you need to convey much more than just the position you held. Always keep in mind that you're not just telling the prospective employer what you did in the past, you're trying to sell them on your abilities—*what you can do for them as an employee*—as it relates to your past experience.

How do you show your potential, as derived from your past experience? The first thing you must do is itemize your responsibilities in whatever jobs you held and activities you participated in. If you were a member of your college debating team, include the responsibilities attached to that membership, and thereby establish your active participation *beyond* the actual debates. Succinctly stated, this technique will tell the prospective employer a lot more about your capabilities and potential.

Whenever you write a résumé, or a cover letter, or have an interview, always remember what the advertising business calls the "you benefit." In other words, relate your experience in terms of benefits for your potential employer. "I can do this for you," "I can do that for you," and so on.

Another important point: when providing a previous job title or related course you took, use some poetic license to make them more descriptive. The reason behind this is that companies have different ways of interpreting the same title. For example, courses often have nondescript titles such as "English 101," which tells very little. You would be much better off by changing it to "Structure, Style, and Composition," if you were to include it on your résumé.

When illuminating your experience, abilities, and responsibilities, *don't be modest.* You should tell the truth and do it positively, and with pride. Think of all the advertisements and commercials you've seen. When advertisers tell you about a product, they are communicating its good points. In addition, they back up their claims with evidence that the product can actually do what they've said. And also, when advertisers try to sell a product, they certainly don't mention any drawbacks they may have discovered about it. But at the same token, in conveying positive attributes, they also have to avoid making the product sound "too good to be true."

Now, this is not to say that you should totally avoid your liabilities, because at some point, they are likely to make themselves known. Avoid mentioning them in a résumé, but be prepared to discuss them in an interview, and in such a way that you are still presented in the most favorable light.

Following the example of advertisements, you should base your own sales campaign on your positive characteristics and accomplishments. A very good way of identifying your accomplishments—while avoiding modesty—is to ask yourself what things would have gone wrong if you hadn't functioned properly in an earlier job, or in a role you held in a club. This is very helpful in the self-examination process required for writing résumés, in that you'll objectively discover what services you have already provided to achieve the goal of an organization. Furthermore, if you were a member of a team that successfully performed a certain duty, then you should take partial credit for that accomplishment. Teamwork is valuable in business, and the fact that you were part of a winning team is not to be overlooked in your résumé.

THE VITAL ELEMENT: SHOWING THE PROSPECTIVE EMPLOYER YOU WANT TO MAKE HIM A PROFIT

Profits make the business world go round, and that should be the underlying theme of your résumé. At all times, you must convey to business people that you are profit motivated. It's easy to ignore the fundamental need for profits, especially if you're just graduating from college. Unless you worked your way through college or studied economics, you probably thought of success more in terms of grades and acquiring knowledge. But remember, even your college couldn't have operated without generating enough money to keep its employees on the payroll and pay the bills.

"Very often, I ask young people how they can contribute to the bottom line of this organization," says one public relations executive. "Ninety-nine out of a hundred times, they can't give me an answer."

What constitutes profits, and how can you show the prospective employer that you're profit-oriented? Profits can be construed in a number of ways: as making money, saving money, saving time, increasing efficiency, and generally contributing to the future of the organization. Have you ever taken the initiative to make sure certain things get done? If you were a member of a college club or community organization, did you bring in new members? Did you provide fund-raising ideas for an organization that were used successfully? If you worked on your college newspaper or literary magazine, did you think of ways to improve the layout or circulation? If you worked at a job, what did you do to generate profits for your company? In nearly every phase of life, you are geared toward some kind of success or accomplishment which, in turn, provided some kind of profit. The more you concentrate on these aspects of your experience and combine them with an overall thrust toward making profits in the business world, the more you will shine above the competition.

Though not always feasible, another way of expressing your interest in increasing the prospective employer's profits is to start training in the media profession of your choice *before* someone hires you. Business people are impressed by applicants who have invested their time, energy, and money in learning about a profession without waiting for on-the-job training. If you take a course in advertising, or study and practice copywriting on your own, that tells a prospective employer a lot. It means that you're not just looking for free training on the job, but shows that your determination to get ahead is strong enough to motivate you to pursue the skills of the profession independently.

"Any time a beginner can show me that he is doing outside work to get ahead, I'll give that person extra consideration," says Marty Cohn of Ogilvy & Mather Direct Response.

It shows that you already know, to a certain degree, what the field is about, and that your decision to have a career in that profession isn't just "fluff." In addition, since you've already gone out and gotten some training in the field, you probably won't require as much on the job—which means a saving in terms of investment of time, energy, and money for the employer—as opposed to other applicants who have not had any formal contact with the profession.

Since your main thrust in getting the prospective employers interested in you is your dedication to increasing their profits, *don't ever state your salary requirements in your résumé.* Even if you're answering a classified advertisement that requests your salary requirements, simply say that salary is "open." You should be concentrating on what you can do for the profits of prospective employers, not what they can do for yours.

CONSTRUCTING THE BASIC ELEMENTS

Now, let's go on to the résumé itself. Included are two good samples (see X and Y) of how you can prepare a résumé. There are many different styles, and no one is considered more correct than another, as long as it contains certain kinds of information.

HEADING

At the top of your résumé always include your name, address, and telephone number where you can be reached. If you are working, then you may include both your home and work number, making sure that they are clearly identified as such. (List your work number only if your boss and co-workers know and approve of your job-hunting, lest you create a very awkward situation for you, your boss, and prospective employers.) Another, more professional way of handling your telephone number is to get an answering service. (You can find one by looking under "answering service" in the Yellow Pages.) Though you may think it's an unnecessary expense and a formality that you can do without, there is no faster way to lose out on a job than by having your prospective employer unable to reach you.

"It drives me crazy to try to track down an applicant," says Risa Bell of Zimmermann Marketing. "If an applicant isn't professional enough to have an answering service, it tells me something about that person. And more than once, I've bypassed a qualified applicant because I couldn't reach him on the phone."

Example X

SHEILA NISSEN

ADDRESS: 12 East 55th Street,
New York, NY 10019.
(212) 555-1234

OBJECTIVE: Account Executive in Advertising

EDUCATION: CORNELL UNIVERSITY: Ithaca, N.Y.
Bachelor of Science, June 1980.
Major: Communication Arts
Scholastic Honors: Dean's List.

CITY OF LONDON POLYTECHNIC:
London, England.
Communications and elective courses,
1/79–6/79.

WORK
EXPERIENCE: SALES ASSISTANT: AMERICAN
BROADCASTING COMPANY.
New York, N.Y.; 10/80–Present.
Recorded and processed syndicated television
program sales orders, prepared station contracts and weekly sales status reports.
Rearranged processing system so information could be covered and comprehended
more quickly, yet more fully, by all
employees. In addition, designed new format
for reports, to state more clearly past performance, while taking into consideration
projected performance for weeks ahead.

ADVERTISING TRAINEE:
STRAND ASSOCIATES.
London, England; 6/79–1/80.
Edited and proofread copy for advertising
brochures, supervised print production traffic,
assisted in client services. Rose from position
of trainee to assistant, handling several clients
in the absence of supervisor.

PART-TIME
EMPLOYMENT: BUSINESS BOARD MEMBER:
                     CORNELL DAILY SUN.
                     Ithaca, N.Y.; 9/76–12/78.
                     Sold advertising space to local merchants,
                     wrote copy and prepared layout of display
                     ads. *Daily Sun*'s income was largest in history
                     of paper, based primarily on advertising
                     sales.

                     COPYWRITER: REIGHTFOLD
                     DESIGN.
                     Cincinnati, Ohio; 6/78–9/78.
                     Wrote copy for catalog of products and
                     services. Sales increased by 10% from
                     previous year.

RELATED
SKILLS: Typing: 55 wpm, and general office skills.
                     Read and speak Italian and Hebrew.

REFERENCES: Furnished upon request.

Example Y

Adele N. Franchi
62 East 75th Street,
New York, NY 10019.
(212) 480-2332

IMMEDIATE
OBJECTIVE: An entry-level position in marketing manage-
                     ment, in the area of research services.

LONG-RANGE
OBJECTIVE: Marketing Research Consultant

EDUCATION:
1975–1979   Hofstra University, School of Business
                     graduated Summa cum Laude with a BBA in
                     Marketing

Concentrated studies in Marketing, Research, Strategy, and Economics

HONORS: Delta Tau Alpha, Hofstra's highest scholastic honorary society
Delta Mu Delta, Hofstra's business honorary society
Trustee Achievement Award, academic scholarship

EXPERIENCE:
1/80–present   Hofstra University
Administrative Assistant, LSAT PREPARATION COURSE: Organized and maintained office, reduced staff by 1 and maintained previous efficiency; assisted Program Recruiter with marketing campaigns, number of participants increased by 12% over previous year; was responsible for library facilities, rearranged library filing system so entire staff could easily retrieve materials.

9/79–1/80   Hofstra University
Administrative Assistant, Financial Development Program: designed and implemented faculty and course evaluations; assembled and analyzed findings; determined advertising sources; organized course materials and assignments.

7/79–8/79   Freelance
Field Interviewer, Manfred Researchers/Today's Youth: interviewed respondents.
Consultant: International Publishers Associates: evaluated media studies.

7/77–6/79   Hofstra University
Student-Aide, Fund Raising Management Program (part-time): performed general clerical work; advanced to assist in administrative services; coordinated and interfaced a marketing research project with Fund Raising's marketing goals; presented a comprehensive

report to Fund Raising Management, which
enabled them to target their market more
accurately; revenue increased by 18% over
prior year.

PERSONAL
DATA: Age: 23   Status: Single

REFERENCES: Will be furnished upon request.

You may also want to put some vital statistics or personal
data in your heading (or if you prefer, at the end of the
résumé). Included here would be a variety of optional items,
such as: age or date of birth, marital status, condition of health,
height and weight. Whether or not to include these statistics is
really a matter of personal taste more than anything else, so if
you're tight for space, leave them out.

SHORT- AND LONG-RANGE OBJECTIVES

Generally speaking, the prospective employer is usually more
interested in an applicant who is goal-directed, than in those
who seem ambiguous about their career direction. Making a decision (or at least appearing to have made a decision) about
what kind of career you want to have in a profession is extremely important in the job-finding process, since you've got to
slant your background to fit your job campaign.

If you have little or no job experience, you probably won't
be hired for the specific job you want. You will probably have
to prove yourself first, in a lesser position, before getting a
crack at a job that has more responsibility. That's fine, since
your main goal at the onset should be to get your foot in the
door. But so you don't get stuck in the same position for the
rest of your life, state both your immediate and long-range career objectives.

"These kids come looking for work, fresh out of college,"
says Richard Sachinis of The Graphic Experience, "and they
think they know it all. As far as I'm concerned, four years of
college counts only for background. Anybody who works for
me, without experience, has got to prove himself. And usually,

that means starting at the bottom and working up. But that's no different from the way we all began."

Besides showing a prospective employer that you're interested in their profession, stating your short- and long-range objectives demonstrates that you are serious about embarking on a career, rather than just getting a job. And beyond that, you're showing them that you've researched their field well enough to know which positions lead to growth, and in what direction. (Part II of this book will help you discover the "tracking" or growth in each profession.) Knowing the tracking in a profession means that you've already spent time learning about the field, and that is something likely to impress the prospective employer.

When you state your short-range objectives, be fairly specific, yet also keep those objectives flexible so as not to limit your options. After all, getting your foot in the door is really the biggest battle you'll encounter when entering the media professions. Therefore, a good way of expressing your short-range objectives is in outline form, such as:

Position as Assistant in Book Publishing, in one of the following areas:

1. Copyediting
2. Editorial
3. Book promotion

That way, you're telling the prospective employer that you'd like to work in an editorial or creative capacity in book publishing, rather than in production, business, or sales.

Next, include your long-range objective. This should show that you're determined to get ahead in the field and that you know what's possible in terms of growth. When stating your long-range objective, you can afford to be somewhat ambiguous, since the position could be five or ten years away. Don't put something as far-reaching as "Editor-in-Chief of Publishing Company" (even though that may be your desire in life), because it is too far off in the future. Rather, you should identify your long-range objective as a position that is a few rungs closer on the ladder, such as editor.

"All the time I have kids tell me they want the president's job," says a senior editor at a publishing house. "I have to laugh, because it's like a phrase they read in a book and they think they'll be 'cool' if that's what they say. I think they sound ridiculous. What kid in his right mind can shoot for the presidency as a result of his first job?"

If you're running short of space on your single-page résumé, don't go to two pages. Find a different, more succinct way of stating your short- and long-range objectives. Though it is not quite as effective as outlining, you could state your objectives with a single sentence. For example:

> "Position as editorial assistant in publishing
> house, leading to full status as book editor."

Again, although this is not quite as effective as outlining your objectives, if you have far more important data to mention in your résumé, approach your career goals with a single sentence.

EDUCATION

If you're just graduating from college (as most people seeking entry-level positions in professions are), you must illuminate your college career to the prospective employer. Rather than going in progressive order, state your degrees or schools attended in reverse chronological order. That means putting the most recent information first, presumably because it has the most bearing on your present qualifications. Put the date on which your degree was awarded (or when you anticipate receiving it), the degree(s) you earned, the college(s) you attended, your major, and your minor if it has relevance. In your section on education, be sure to include any awards or scholarships you may have won. They are endorsements of your learning achievements.

Include any major research projects or theses you worked on, especially if they are relevant to your future profession. Even if they have little or no bearing on the field, you should still mention them, since they are accomplishments, but don't go into great detail when describing them.

If you are enrolled in any profession-related courses right now, mention them in your résumé. In fact, if they're the only profession-related contact that you have, put those courses right at the top of your education section. It could be the thing that gets you an interview!

EXPERIENCE

Even if you've never had a job, you can still present a strong section about your experience. Sometimes it is helpful to break this section into two parts. If you've had some experience (whether paid or volunteer) in your chosen field, then separate that from other work experience so it stands out in tandem with your stated goal. If, for instance, you would like to go into advertising and have worked for the past two summers in an advertising-related capacity, then you could isolate this by placing it under the heading, "Advertising Experience." Other paid or volunteer work experience could then be put under the separate heading, "Other Experience."

"Someone's got to give a break-inner a first job," says Annette Swanstrom, Vice-President, Prescott Lists, "and I'm happy to consider a person with no experience. But his or her résumé had better communicate that that person has an awful lot on the ball, and the same with the interview."

As you did with your education section, list your job experience in reverse chronological order, that is, your most recent activity first.

How to Describe Your Experience   When writing up your job experience, just stating the name of the company you worked for and the position you held is not enough. It doesn't illustrate to the prospective employer what you actually did, nor does it show what you're capable of doing for them. To provide a clear, accurate picture of your work experience, you must describe the major functions you performed as an employee. Itemize your full responsibilities in the job, and then pare them down until you've consolidated the most important duties you performed. It will tell the prospective employer a lot about your capabilities. And whatever you do, make sure that the experience you include in some way *indicates* that you are *profit-oriented*. Overlooking this is one of the biggest mistakes that is made on all résumés, and on all levels. Not enough people think in terms of profits, but if you do, it's a sure way to give yourself a competitive edge.

To describe your job responsibilities effectively, you've got to think long and hard about your past jobs. What did you actually do on a day-to-day basis? What did you get done? How did you handle your responsibilities? Were you commended by your employer? Did you make sure everything in your area ran smoothly? Were you able to make or save money for the company? Time? Were you responsible for any other people on the job? How did you function in that capacity? What valuable skills did you acquire on the job? Now, for each job, take your answers from these questions and condense them into one or two lines that spotlight your major job responsibilities.

ACTIVITIES

This section presents miscellaneous items such as your interests, hobbies, and clubs or organizations in which you participated both in and out of school. It not only presents a fuller picture of you as a person, but also can provide some ice-breaking conversation during an interview. If you have won any awards or held any office in your outside activities, mention it here along with the duties that you performed.

SKILLS

Generally, skills are placed near the bottom of the résumé. They would include typing (if yours is under 50 words per minute, omit your speed, since it could work against you), shorthand or speedwriting, knowledge of business machines like dictaphone, qwip, or telex, and any other specialized office skills, such as bookkeeping.

Many young people just embarking on careers, refrain from describing their skills, especially typing, in their résumés. They fear it will get them stuck in the secretarial pool for the rest of their business life. The fact is, however, it's very likely that it

will be your typing and other clerical skills that get you your
first job. So be sure to mention your skills, and if you get an interview, tell the person you're willing to *start* your career as a
secretary.

Times have changed. The number of entry-level positions
has substantially decreased in the last decade and so have the
opportunities to start in a trainee position and rise to the top of
the company. If you seriously want to break into the media professions, then you must be willing to take almost anything as
your first job. Once you've done that, then you can begin to
prove yourself to your employer. This means that you could
be hired as a typist or a secretary and then move up. Indeed,
since so many companies look to fill responsible positions from
within, almost any job represents a real career opportunity.
Your biggest battle is getting your first job, so don't limit the
possibilities.

In the media professions, more than in any other field, typing
is very often a necessity. Even the people who have risen high
enough to have secretaries working for them still do some of
their own typing. After all, many of the crafts in the media
profession depend on the spontaneity of typing to express ideas
and information.

There is a major advertising agency in New York whose account executives are almost all women. When a senior manager
was questioned about this, he replied: "Many young people,
both men and women, have asked me for advice on how to
break into advertising. I've told them all to start as secretaries
and then work their way up. It seems that only the women lis-
tened to my advice!"

REFERENCES

Even if you've never had a job, you still can provide some
very valuable references. Many people think that the only valid
kind of reference comes from paid employment, but that's not
true. Generally, there are three types of references: work-
related (paid or volunteer), academic, and personal.

If you've ever had a job, worked well, and had a good relationship with your boss, you should include work-related references. This is especially true if you had a job related to your chosen field in the media professions. Of course, before you supply anyone's name as a reference, discuss it with them.

"If a person has had any kind of paid work experience, I want to speak with the employer if at all possible," says another personnel director. "It's just one more way of checking out the person."

When including your work-related references, you can place them either at the end of your résumé or next to your job-experience entries. If you do place them in your Experience section, write "Reported to Mr. John Jones," next to your job entry.

If you are a recent college graduate, be sure to get at least two written recommendations from your professors. Most colleges will hold them on file for you, so that you or the prospective employer can request them. Incidentally, if given the choice, you—not the prospective employer—should be the one to request the references from your college, since you want to be as helpful as possible in getting yourself hired.

Personal references are the least important of all references, since in most cases they endorse you as a trustworthy friend or nice neighbor, as opposed to a good worker. Use character references only when they're requested, and be wary of name-dropping by using an influential name in your chosen field in a character reference capacity. The way to include references in your résumé is to write, at the bottom, "References will be furnished upon request."

MAKING THE RÉSUMÉ LOOK DISTINCTIVE

Having spent so much time refining the content of your résumé, you don't want a prospective employer to overlook you because of a sloppy, dull, or otherwise visually unappealing presentation of your résumé. Furthermore, since your résumé could be one in a pile of a thousand or more, don't get "lost in the crowd" by being indistinguishable from all the others.

Therefore, your next job is to create a clean, professional, and conservative résumé that *stands out*.

PAPER SIZE

Your first consideration should be the size of paper you are planning to use. Don't let your résumé look barren of content or overwhelming, in terms of the amount of print on the page. (See Samples X and Y in reference to what kind of spacing you should use.)

There are three paper sizes which are most commonly considered appropriate for résumés. 8½″ x 11″ is the most common, and fits neatly into a stack of other résumés (most files are made for that size, too).

Monarch size paper (7″ x 10″) does stand out, since it is smaller than the 8½″ x 11″ stock, but because of its decreased size, it could get lost in a stack. In addition, it doesn't give you very much space for the content of your résumé. In concept, legal-size paper (8½″ x 14″) is the best, since it sticks out in a stack of résumés and gives you a large amount of space to work with. But because of its oversized dimensions, legal-size paper should usually be avoided, unless you've got something important to say.

ENVELOPE SIZE

Most people send their résumés out in a standard #10 (4⅛″ x 9½″) envelope, since it conforms with the professional conventions of business. Other options include a 6″ x 9″ envelope, which would require you to fold your 8½″ x 11″ résumé in half, or a 9″ x 12″ envelope, which would allow you to send out your résumé flat and unfolded. Whatever your envelope choice, make sure it matches the paper that you've chosen for your résumé. In addition, if you decide to use a 9″ x 12″ mailing envelope, you should adhere address labels with your name and address typed on them. It makes for a more professional look. *Do not hand address any envelope.*

PAPER STOCK

When you've determined the size of paper you plan to use for your résumé, you then must decide on the stock. Your considerations here should be the color, weight, and texture of the paper, and you should look for something that varies slightly from the norm.

There are many colors other than plain white that are available in paper stocks, and you should look into them. In varying from the norm, yet still retaining a professional look, you should consider such colors as light gray, buff, ivory, or a brilliant white. Stay away from dark or even medium colors, since they don't show the type as well. Also avoid pastel colors, since they are not considered professional.

Check the weight of your paper stock carefully. You don't want to purchase paper that is so lightweight that it feels flimsy. Nor do you want it to be translucent, due to insubstantial bulk. Also avoid a very heavy stock, because it cracks when you fold it and often demands extra postage. The best paper weight for a résumé is generally 24-pound bond, but because of different methods in manufacturing, this same weight of paper is sometimes called 60-pound offset. This is a good, sturdy stock and you would do well to use it.

Your next consideration should be the texture of your paper. Though it is optional, if you do look into it, you must use something conservative. A lightly textured paper, with a laid, cambric, or parchment finish, can add a nice touch to your résumé. When you rub the paper between your fingers, you can feel the texture. This indicates a better quality stock. A good, conservative textured paper is worth using, because it will play a part in making a positive impression on the prospective employer.

PRINT

The aim of putting your résumé on a distinctive-looking stock is to attain a clean, professional look, and you must keep that same goal in mind when you put the actual words down on

the paper. Avoid using a manual typewriter, or a typewriter
with a cloth or nylon ribbon, because they tend to print un-
evenly. If you plan to type every copy of your résumé, you
should use an electric typewriter with a "mylar" (a kind of
plastic) ribbon, which produces a clean, clear, black type. All
letters look even, and it is easy to read.

*There is nothing more unimpressive to a prospective em-
ployer than an obvious copy (either carbon or photostat) of a
résumé. It's unprofessional and it looks as if you don't care
about getting the job.*

If you have your résumé printed professionally, you will
have a choice of several different typefaces. (Typeface is the
term for the particular style of lettering and you'll notice that
magazines, newspapers, and printed advertisements use all
different styles of letters in their printing.) You need a typeface
that's easy to read, and you should ask for advice from your
printer. Selecting a typeface that resembles typewriter type is
fine since it assures a conservative, professional-looking résumé.
In addition, make sure that the typeface is big enough to read,
such as 10- or 12-point type, standard for typewriters.

PROOFREADING

Before typing or having your résumé printed, you must make
sure it is as close to perfection as possible.

1. Check it over, and have someone else do it, too, to
   catch any spelling or grammatical errors and refine
   your word usage.
2. Make sure your résumé is readable on the basis of
   comprehension. Avoid using any big, impressive words
   unless they're absolutely necessary, and try to find replacement words for technical jargon. If you have repeated certain words frequently, find synonyms for
   them. A thesaurus is helpful in such cases, but make
   sure you understand both the meaning and connotation
   of the replacement word before you use it.
3. Check your résumé for style and make sure it follows
   the rules of verb tense agreement. If you've stated your
   job duties in one area of your résumé in the past tense,

and state your activities in the present tense in another, then change it. All verbs must either be in the present or the past tense, *throughout* the résumé.

4. Make sure the entire résumé has been written for the intended audience. Every word and every idea must be absolutely clear. Spell out all abbreviations unless they're absolutely necessary, and then only if they will be completely understood. Keep in mind that you're out to impress people with your accomplishments, not boggle their minds!

TESTING YOUR RÉSUMÉ

Before you go through the expense of having your résumé printed, test it to know that it is effective. Type up several copies and send them out in response to classified advertisements, and show them to your friends and people you know in business. Get their comments and suggestions on how to improve it.

When you discover that your résumé really does work, that it does obtain interviews, then, and only then, should you have it printed. A résumé that triggers response is the only kind to have printed up, or else you'll have spent time and money for nothing.

Now, with résumé in hand, it's time for the interview—the most important step in finding that media job of your choice.

Chapter 5

THE INTERVIEW: BE PREPARED!

WHY THE INTERVIEW IS SO IMPORTANT

Getting an interview is the most important step towards obtaining a job. The company has to talk with you, *and accept you,* before the job is yours. On the other hand, the interview allows you to receive the information that helps decide *whether you want* to accept the job and work for that company. It's an inquiring and negotiating process. You have to sell yourself to the company and its representatives, but they have to make themselves desirable to you too.

It is not unusual for you to be interviewed by more than one person. Several interviews may be needed as you come closer to acceptance and a job-offer. This route of successive interviews is employed by companies to select the right individual for the job. Each interviewer knows what duties have to be performed in the position to be filled, the salary that can be paid, and the variety of qualifications which must be considered. Picking the right applicant is a boost to an organization; hiring the wrong applicant can be costly in time, money, and bad experiences.

"For every job opening available, I'll bet we have at least twelve to fifteen people who really deserve the job," Malcolm Smith, Vice-President, Ventura Associates, says. "It's a tough decision to make. And when it comes right down to making the choice, we've got to look deeper than just grades and course of study. Are they willing to work hard? How do they respond to the questions in the interview? Were they on time? Were they dressed appropriately? And most importantly, did they know anything about our company—did they take the time to find out about us, and how they might make a contribution? We look for all those things in a candidate."

Any decisions made by the executive and you, during the interview, can affect both the company and yourself for years. Your letters of recommendation, résumé, application form, school grades or diploma, samples of your work, and list of previous experiences just help the interviewers to form an opinion, but the interview itself is what prompts the decision. Despite whatever contact that may have gotten you this far, *you don't have the job until the interviewing process is finished,* the job has been offered to you, and you choose to accept it.

There are different interview structures in reaching the final job-offer, at different companies. Many organizations start with a low-level person, who screens people according to instructions and then passes likely candidates up to a higher-level decision-maker. In other situations, several people give interviews and combine their opinions. This allows different interviewers to pick up on factors that others may have missed. Still another procedure is the panel-interview, in which one person is chairperson and other concerned individuals are present to listen and ask questions. And, of course, there is always the situation where the person doing the hiring can make a conclusion in the first conversation, give all the details, and offer you the job on the spot. You could encounter any one of these interviewing procedures, but don't panic. *Just be prepared.*

You can improve your chances of success on an interview, if you know and understand what you'll encounter. You wouldn't buy a car without knowing something about its good points, potential problems, and capabilities. You have to live with that car for a long time, so the automobile had better fill enough of your expectations and needs, or you will be very unhappy by your choice. The dealer wants to sell a particular car to you, and you are willing to be convinced—thus the questions you ask and the way the salesperson answers them play an essential part in making the decision whether you'll buy the car.

The company interviewing you is in the same situation. All applicants must be looked over and questioned, in order to make the best choice possible. The company's smooth functioning, growth, and financial strength lie in the capabilities of its staff, and the interviewing process is for selecting good staff members. You want to be the person asked to join the company, so you must supply enough favorable answers and reasons to prove why you should be the one chosen for the job.

"It's a corporate policy to hire from within whenever possible," says a major executive at a large publishing company. "So the people you hire, even at the entry level, need to have the capabilities to move up. Continuity of staff is one of the ways a company prospers and grows. That's why every candidate is carefully screened."

The selection of a new employee is normally made up of four steps:

1. Applying for the job
2. The screening interview
3. The selection interview
4. The job-offer interview

Sometimes these steps are combined. Other times, one phase can consist of several interviews with different people. The procedure is based on the job to be filled, the number of applicants, the needs of the company, and the individual reactions of the people you will be involved with if you are hired. Beyond some general ideas, you can't be sure there are any "right" answers to the questions that will be asked. Every interviewer and executive responds differently, and has his or her own reasons for reaching conclusions.

THE APPLICATION

To be considered for hiring, the company has to know whether it is worth the time and effort to go through the numerous steps needed to find out if you are appropriate for the job—particularly since a lot of other people are probably seeking that job too. So, they ask you to fill out an application form. This asks questions which reveal to them whether you are even in the ball park, insofar as the position to be filled is concerned. Your answers on this form may even suggest that you would fit into another slot, one that you or the company had not initially considered.

Application forms provide the prospective employer with information that résumés generally do not explore. A résumé is beneficial and is often required, but the company may have its own application form, and for its own good set of reasons. The company wants as much information about the applicant as is reasonably possible to obtain, in writing, before it proceeds. From the applications and résumés, the interviewer determines who seems to be seriously worth considering. Some people will be candidates for in-depth screening, others will be interviewed only as a courtesy and the remainder will get a brief "Thanks, we'll keep your name on file if an opening develops," and won't even get past the front desk.

Never, never take an application form lightly. Simply stated, it is one key way a company makes a judgment about you. Naturally, you want your application to be neat. If necessary, scribble notes for your answers on a separate sheet, and then copy them down on the application. Make your answers succinct and meaningful. This will be a lot easier to do for the person who has spent the time to assess him or herself, and is aware of the ways in which corporate contributions can be made. If you are not satisfied with the answers you have given on one application, jot down the questions in your notebook, and later work out better answers. If necessary, have someone review your answers. It is very likely that you will come across similar types of questions on other applications.

WHAT THE INTERVIEWER WILL LOOK FOR ON YOUR APPLICATION AND RÉSUMÉ

Completed applications, supporting papers, and résumés are usually evaluated by such things as experience, progress, stability, and how you follow directions. Interviewers make allowance for some factors that may have been beyond your control, and you'll probably be invited to comment on those things deserving explanation.

1. *Experience:* Your work experience and exposure to different types of situations in various phases of your life carry weight in any decision. Often, the things you did apart from the job have just as much value as your previous employment background.

2. *Progress:* The pattern of your experience shows if you have been moving forward. In any jobs held, the salaries received and the duties performed reveal your increasing ability to handle assigned tasks and take on responsibility. School subjects, areas of interest, and involvement in extracurricular activities provide insight about your tendencies and natural inclinations. Even if your job and other experiences are not applicable to the job for which you are applying, they do show your outlook, self-motivation, ability to stick to a task, determination, and other important qualities.

   "I like people who know what they want," Ed Cooperman, Vice-President and Marketing Director for the Gold Card, American Express, says. "That's one of the reasons I prefer people who have their MBA. It shows they actually studied further in a particular subject area. If people don't have their MBA," Ed Cooperman continues, "then I like for them to find some way to show me that they have specific interests."

3. *Stability:* If you changed courses frequently, switched schools, moved from job to job, or had frequent geographical relocations, it may indicate to the potential employer that you want to make changes, even on the new job for which you are applying. It could be troublesome and time-consuming to replace you, if you left the position soon, but on the other hand, indicating that you would be steadfast in one position could be interpreted as timidity in facing new conditions, or in making tough decisions that may be involved in altering your direction. You can't be sure how the interviewer will respond to the summary you give. If there is a question about something like this, you will hear it asked during your interview. Otherwise, don't volunteer excuses or explanations. They could open doors you would prefer remained closed. The kinds of questions

asked by the interviewer can serve as important clues to what they are thinking. Once again, make notes after the interview, of the kinds of questions that were asked. Was there a pattern? If so, be prepared to answer those questions in the future, and in such a way that they show you to the best advantage.

4. *Following directions:* If you are unable to fill out the application form neatly, coherently, and completely as in accordance with instructions, the potential employer may wonder if you will also have trouble following directions on the job. *Complete your application form exactly as requested.*

Your application form and résumé will be read before any interview or questioning begins. Expect to see notations on what you have written, for these indicate things that are significant to the interviewer, and may be the basis for the questions you'll be asked.

A CHECKLIST FOR THE SCREENING INTERVIEW

After submitting your application and résumé, if you are invited in for an interview, you've passed the first hurdle! *You would not have been invited to the talk if you were not being considered for the job.*

To make a good personal impression, you must be aware of some key factors. You are seeking a job and need to do a good job in selling yourself. Some steps to help in doing that are:

BE ON TIME!

"There's nothing more aggravating than the candidate who shows up late for an interview," says Jim Pettijohn, Marketing Manager, Citibank. "In fact, unless they have an incredibly good reason for their lateness, I generally consider that to be an indication of how they feel about getting the job."

Jim Pettijohn isn't the only executive who feels this way. Lateness seems to be a pet peeve in general. So, take this as a warning. *Allow ample time to get to your interview.* And if you arrive too early, then pass the time at a coffee shop and use those moments as an opportunity for last-minute preparation.

APPEARANCE

Be dressed and groomed neatly, as befitting the company interviewing you and the job you are seeking. *Look like a winner.* With a distinguished, highly reputable firm, you automatically strike out if you walk in wearing blue jeans. No tie, beat-up shoes, wrinkled or frayed clothes, or unkempt hair are all elements that cause an immediate, negative reaction.

"I once interviewed a very nice woman who showed up in a tailored blouse, denim skirt and a knock-around jacket," says Annette Swanstrom of Prescott Lists. "Somehow, her incredibly casual dress, combined with her attitude, led me to believe that she really didn't aspire to do much if she worked for us. I want people to look the part of the job they want—not the one they are being hired for."

Dress neatly and conservatively, with a plain shirt or dress rather than something loud. Never wear faddish clothing. Wear clothes that fit you well and make you look and feel good. Dress for the job you want.

PREPARATION

Have anything that may be called for with you. This includes a pen or pencil, notepaper, school transcript, diploma, résumé, samples of work you've done, letters of commendation, and anything else you think will prove your sincerity of purpose to the interviewer.

"Coming to an interview prepared, and that means paper, pen, résumé, samples of work, etc., is just one more example of a person who really wants a job," says Malcolm Smith of Ventura Associates. "And all these little things eventually add up and help one person stand out from the rest."

DESIRE

Know what you want. Have a goal or a job that you desire, one that can be described easily, quickly, and clearly. If responding to a specific advertisement, be ready to explain why that work would appeal to you. You must say why you'd like to work for the organization interviewing you. Be ready with answers telling how you might contribute qualities and abilities that could be beneficial for the company. Wait until asked, however, before heading into such comments.

"Remember, when you go into any interviews for entry-level positions, or any positions," says Tom Moore, President of Tomorrow Entertainment, "you should make it clear that you know what you want—even if you're not really sure. You can't just go in and say, 'Well, I want to work in the film industry for a year or two to see what I want to do.' It's the fastest way to kill an interview."

FIRST GREETING

You may be brought into the interviewer's office, or the individual may come out to you. Either way, give a firm, enthusiastic, pleasant handshake and greeting. Be the first one to make a statement, if possible, after the first hello. Compliment the interviewer on something about the company or on a subject that shows you have prepared yourself for this interview.

GIVE-AND-TAKE

Your ability to respond to the personality of the interviewer is important. Just relax, be yourself, and remember that you are dealing with a human being. That individual has personal ways of functioning, just as you do. Adjust yourself to the person and situation as best you can. Having a good exchange of information and being responsive to the interviewer, is a vital part of making a good impression. Putting the interviewer on the defensive, breaking a train of thought, or ignoring signals will work against you.

"I have interviewed many people who have talked themselves right out of a job," says Bob DeLay, President, Direct Mail/Marketing Association. "In fact, one time I was interviewing a woman and she should have known that she had the job by the comments I made. But she just kept on talking and

talking and talking and finally I interrupted her and told her
that if she wanted the job, she should really *stop* talking."

You can't force yourself to be someone other than who and
what you are. Yet, displaying self-confidence and stimulating a
good discussion during an interview, should help you consid-
erably. Being *honest, sincere,* and *enthusiastic* are the important ingredients in a successful job conversation.

Courtesy

Let the interviewer do the talking and questioning. You'll get
your chance to mention your own thoughts when the time
comes. Make notes, if necessary, to remind yourself about
questions.

Play It Cool

By showing you are anxious for the job, you undercut your
bargaining position. It also displays a lack of self-confidence.
This might cost you salary, side benefits, and flexibility, if the
job is actually offered. By a soft-sell approach, you will be in
the lead when the potential employer starts pursuing you.

On the other hand, you don't want to play it so cool that the
interviewer feels that you aren't really interested. *Be cool, but
also be enthusiastic.* Again, if you have researched the company
and the type of position, it's a lot easier to be naturally enthusiastic, and at the same time, somewhat reserved.

Tell the Truth

Supply answers to questions without feeling you must defend
yourself. There are numerous ways of answering the same question, so pick the most positive, self-assured one. Don't volunteer answers about your background that might count against
you. Of course, if you are asked, you should reply, but know
ahead of time how you will respond.

Here again is where your notebook can come in handy. If
you feel that you fielded a difficult question especially well, jot
down your answer after the interview. Conversely, if you felt

uncomfortable with your response, note that too, and then figure out the ways you could have truthfully answered the question and put yourself in a good light.

AMBITIONS

Tailor-fit your approach to the position for which you are applying. Describe your dedication to your work and to any project in which you have been involved. Demonstrate that you have the inner drive to do the work that is being discussed and have an example ready. It's okay to say you have higher goals for the future, but also say you are willing to stay with the job being discussed for the length of time as best fulfills the needs of the company. However, you should add, you'd be open to any training or up-grading program of the firm, as it becomes appropriate. Indicate, if asked, that you're willing to put in "a year or so" at the job, if chances for advancement exist after that time and you have proven yourself deserving of them. By saying this, the interviewer will, at least, feel that a substitute for your job wouldn't be needed in just a few weeks' time.

KNOWLEDGE

Learn about your prospective employer from every source possible: magazines, newspapers, trade publications, contacts or government publications. Publicly owned firms have annual reports and other information available. You'll make a strong impression if you *ask questions or make comments regarding the company's growth, its place in the industry, or its sales potential.*

"Do the homework," one broadcast executive says. "Read the annual report, talk to a stock broker. That way, you can learn about the company and its profit picture. And if you know that, you're bound to favorably impress your interviewer."

OBSERVE AND LISTEN WELL

By keeping your eyes and ears open, you will get a feeling

about the company, its people, and its operations. You are indicating a willingness to devote part of your life to that organization, so the company has to sell itself to you too. So in addition to trying to sell yourself to the interviewer, let that person
talk and listen carefully to what is being said. You also can
learn a lot by asking a question such as, "Who held the job
previously?" and "Did they move to another job in the company?"

QUESTIONS ASKED OF YOU

Your application and résumé have given most of the factual
information. But these do not tell *why* something happened, or
why you responded the way you did. Here is your chance to explain some of the reasons and factors involved. Often the interviewer is most interested in your attitude, and your relationship
with your job and with the people with whom you have been in
contact. Looking at your papers, a question may arise, such as
"How would you evaluate the supervisor on your summer
job?" Or, "Tell me about the ability of the coach and the cap-
tain on your school team." Your replies will reveal whether you
are critical or understanding, at war with the world and blame
others for whatever happens, or whether you followed orders
even if you disagreed with them. Other questions reveal answers about the way you function.

The purpose of the questions is not to trick you, but always
take great care in answering them. Suppose you have changed
courses or major directions frequently in the past. The interviewer might ask you if it is worth spending a lot of training
effort on you, when you are prone to changing directions. You
must then have a good explanation for the events and grades
shown in your records, and present adequate and reassuring
reasons for the changes made.

Don't try to hide facts, but don't overexplain either. Put
yourself in the position of an interviewer. How would you respond to the answers you are about to supply? Allow for
broad-mindedness and a willingness to understand, but also re-

alize that a positive, well-explained answer will be much better received than an evasion, mumbling, or weak excuses.

Questions You Ask

Somewhere during the interview you will be asking questions and interviewers often encourage them. They help to provide a clear picture of the company and factors that deserve exploration. Make sure your questions are career oriented, or you may turn the interviewer off. For example, if you show special interest in the company's policy on vacations, salary improvement procedures, and holidays, you are telegraphing to the interviewer that you don't have an overwhelming concern about the job potential, or the specific information that a forward-looking and career-bound applicant would typically ask for.

"The biggest turn-off to me," says Suzanne Roper, Account Supervisor, Ogilvy & Mather Direct Response, "is the person who asks about the company's benefits right up front. At this stage of their careers, they shouldn't care about perks, they should care about the opportunity to learn."

Suzanne Roper isn't alone in her feeling. According to the media executives interviewed, being asked about "benefits" early on in the interview is a big turn-off. *They want people who are interested in learning and performing on the job,* not those who want to know how many vacation days a year they are going to get.

Job-seekers who have more to offer the company than others, might ask about training offered on the job, specific details about the duties, technical matters concerning the work, and what areas the company is trying to advance in that might relate to the job, but detailed answers are not necessarily given. At the moment, the interviewer may not be at liberty to reply fully to what you ask. But the nature of your questions can distinguish you from a routine applicant. And, if you have researched the company, you will be able to ask questions like these intelligently and constructively.

SALARY

The subject will come up during the first interview. Information will probably be provided in general terms, giving you some idea of the salary range, with the interviewer keyed in on your reaction. Detailed discussions usually do not occur until the job is offered to you. If you are asked, try to avoid a precise reply. You might say, "In the $_____" area, or "Between $_____ and $_____, based on the needs and responsibilities of the work." Or, say the salary is "open" and subject to discussion.

A word of advice: *If you really want to get into the media professions, it is usually best to say the salary is open. Starting salaries tend to be very low, and if you request a particular salary level, you are likely to price yourself out of the ball park. Remember, your main task is to break in at whatever level you can and then work like crazy and volunteer for assignments to get ahead.* As Bob DeLay of the Direct Mail/Marketing Association put it: "After all, who could turn away a worker who is assertive and responsible and looks for additional work?"

It is an acknowledged fact that starting media job salaries are below many other fields, but as a young hopeful (who is now a very successful advertising executive) once said: "Working for _____ & _____ is like working for the Peace Corps—you get paid nothing, but the satisfaction, the creative stimuli that come from working with great creative people—well, you just can't buy that."

EDUCATION

You may be blessed in having the right education in the right subject with just the right amount of training. The odds are generally against it though. So how does the interviewer plug your educational background into the decision-process when hiring?

Frequently, people are hired who have sufficient training to get started, with the understanding that they take additional training while employed. Sometimes this includes company training, other times the firm will ask you or even pay for you to attend outside courses. Many organizations spend thousands of dollars training and up-grading their personnel, because they know that nothing remains static. There are always new challenges and new areas of knowledge to conquer. So lacking some of the educational areas desired by the company does not automatically exclude you from consideration.

As a matter of fact, having straight As doesn't necessarily give an applicant the edge over those with lower grades. Such things as personality, manners, attitude, ambition, knowledge of certain subjects, willingness, potentials for progressing within the company—any of these things may be given stronger consideration than a high scholastic average.

NERVOUSNESS

Most job applicants are uneasy. It shows in many ways, such as mumbling, nodding nervously, tapping fingers on knees or table, or removing glasses frequently. Interviewers do their best to make you feel at ease. They know you are tense. But the more prepared you are for the interview, the less likelihood your nervousness will get in the way. Many people feel that it is good to be nervous before an interview. It shows that you care and gets your adrenalin going. That's good. But if nervous mannerisms overshadow your interviews, then you'd better investigate methods of toning them down.

TALKATIVE APPLICANTS

Watch out that you don't talk excessively or elaborate on information in such detail that the interviewer's attention drifts. The applicant who answers every question with a dissertation or lengthy excuse can find the interview being ended quickly. While too much talking sometimes indicates nervousness, behind which lies real talent, there are applicants who tell one story after another, to avoid giving an answer or to hide a lack of certain qualifications. Most often, it shows a lack of preparation. Let the interviewer run the show—with, of course, a little help from you in pointing out your special capabilities and strengths.

AVOID PRESSURING

You'll be headed for trouble if you try creating an artificial squeeze by citing offers received from other places, especially competitive organizations. If you indicate that the firm will lose a good applicant unless it takes you, a good interviewer will then probe in such a way that not only finds the truth, but quickly latches onto vague statements that you cannot specifically back up. Being aggressive is useful, but putting on pressure in this competitive job market will probably be your undoing.

DON'T ATTACK

If you try to overwhelm, bulldoze, or snow the interviewer, you'll be caught at it, and quickly. Putting a company representative on the defensive has a bad effect and the interviewer will generally turn thumbs down on such an applicant. This includes people who are prone to arguing about differences of opinion—this is an interview, not a debate.

THE PURPOSE OF THE INTERVIEW

The purpose of the first interview is to screen out applicants who do, or do not, meet basic requirements. Fifteen minutes is the typical time allotted to determine these facts. It is in this session that the interviewer asks for elaboration on certain information. This is the conversation for the interviewer to get a feel as to whether the applicant has promise.

This first interview is crucial. It is on this interview that it will be determined whether or not you are invited back. And since, generally, the time allotted for this initial interview is so short, you've got to make every moment count. That's why your preparation is so important. *Know what you're going to say and how you are going to say it.* Use the chance to favorably impress the interviewer, and don't put yourself in the position of having to stumble for an answer.

"I want my staff to have higher ambitions," says Jim Pettijohn of Citibank, "but I also want to feel that they are going to stay with the job for which they are being interviewed for a reasonable length of time. If a candidate spends his time talking about what he or she can do for me in the future, I'm not particularly interested. I want to know what they can do for the company *now*."

Note-taking by the interviewer is to be expected. It is not intended to get you up-tight or put you on your guard. Important conclusions could be forgotten by the time the final selection of the applicant is made, and sometimes other executives rely on those remarks when making their own evaluation. In fact, you should consider the interview to be going fairly well if the interviewer is taking notes. Most times, a person in whom they have little interest makes it unnecessary to take a lot of notes. A simple "not suitable" will do.

Hundreds of different forms and procedures exist throughout the hiring-offices of the nation. One typical method is to have a work-sheet and checklist filled out by anyone who interviews you. These are compared and reviewed. On the form, four main columns might be at the top: Outstanding, Acceptable, Unacceptable, and Comments. Room for notes or check marks are provided alongside such questions as:

- Does this person have the basic experience needed for the job?

- Is the basic education or training acceptable?

- Does applicant have special skills needed for the job?

- Can the individual meet the special working conditions of the job?

- Is applicant's appearance and dress right for job and company?

- (Other questions, relative to attitude, personality, ability to communicate, imagination, ingenuity, self-motivation

—anything might be included in the form, based on what
is significant to the company and the job it wants to fill.)

OTHER AREAS THE INTERVIEW COVERS

FOLLOWING ORDERS

The interviewer wants to find out whether you are a person
who follows instructions, or resents them. A question designed
to reveal your outlook might be one that asks you to describe
and evaluate your supervisor in a previous job, or a leading executive of the school, college, or university you attended. Your
reply will indicate the type of leadership to which you best respond, and whether you adhered to rules, though you might
have disagreed with them. If your descriptions and attitudes
differ from the company's outlook, you could have problems. A
firm knows that all orders aren't well received by employees,
but it can't afford to have major or even minor mutinies within
its ranks.

ATTITUDES

How you feel about your work is important. Typical question: "What did you like best, or least, about your last job?"
Was it a drag, was it just to earn money, or did you gain satisfaction in achieving results? The interviewer can learn much
from your answer. Happy, contented workers are, of course, a
pleasure to have in operating a company, particularly those
who enjoy coming to work and producing good results.

IDEA DEVELOPMENT

Are you inventive, capable of coming up with new ideas and
techniques? In certain media jobs, this is the key to success. In
other duties, it is appreciated, but not essential. If being good at
creating new ideas and bringing them to fruition is a forte of
yours, bring up the subject, when appropriate, and have examples ready to back up your statement.

WORKING WITH OTHERS

If you have difficulty relating to others, or working well with them, everyone involved may be headed for trouble. Some executives maintain that "team-efforts" and inter-relationships are an important element of good company functioning. To others, it warrants little consideration in making their decision. Know where you stand personally. In all likelihood, your response to something you are asked will communicate how you relate to others.

CRITICISM

Your ability to give and accept criticism is a vital part of many creative media jobs. Better results are usually achieved when a person is open to comments and suggestions. If you are touchy about being criticized, you are better off seeking a different kind of job, one where your sensibilities won't get ruffled too easily by being exposed to others' comments.

STRENGTHS AND WEAKNESSES

Sometimes a job applicant has a weakness, or lack of certain qualities that are desired for the job that is open. Yet, there may be compensating factors. Don't give up hope because you don't score well in certain areas of questioning. The interviewer does not necessarily draw conclusions the same way and for the same reasons that you do. Sometimes, a less qualified candidate is selected because of possessing certain traits or training which may be important in unannounced company plans for the future.

Although these interview question areas and others that you are likely to encounter, are not always easy to respond to, you should bear in mind that an interviewer does not expect you to answer them as if you have had years of experience.

Lack of job experience is not necessarily a deterrent to interviewers, and that's why there are so many other points of consideration. Other data must be compiled and subjective opinions must be made. That's also why high grades and special talent don't count for everything in the media job market. *Remember, there is always something you can do to tip the scales in your favor.*

CAREER POTENTIAL

For jobs that are a start in a media career and may eventually lead you up the ladder in the organization, areas explored in the interview could include the following, but keep in mind that the company is considering taking you in as a trainee, not as a vice-president!:

- *Maturity in Thinking:* Do you have realistic goals for yourself? Your attitude toward work and your judgment expressed in answering some problems cited by the interviewer, can give a clue about your thinking processes.

- *Resourcefulness:* Some people are better than others in tackling and coping with challenges, and this skill is essential for positions of responsibility. If you don't know an answer, instead of guessing, ask the interviewer who you could go to for advice. And sometimes it is better to say you would consult experts, rather than try to do all the problem-solving on the job yourself.

- *Pressures:* On the job, some tasks will require fast responses and quick decisions, while at the same time, other duties will flood you with work that must be done within a specified time limit. The speed in which you reply to the interviewer's questions may indicate how well you can think and respond under pressure.

- *Analytical:* If you give a quick reply to a complex question, you are either a genius, or, more likely, you are making an error. Being thoughtful and analytical produces a better answer and a better acceptance of it by the interviewer, rather than a quick, off-the-cuff reply that really needs more elaboration.

- *Assertiveness:* If you get a question such as "Have you ever been in a situation where you worked out your own way of getting things done and had others agree to it?"

the interviewer will learn a lot more about you by the time you have finished your answer. Showing drive, and doing it in such a way that results are achieved with enthusiasm and cooperation, will score points for you.

PROBLEM QUESTIONS

Once you have been on a few interviews, you will begin to see that a number of questions asked by interviewers are not easy to answer. Make sure you take note of them, so that in the future, you can be better prepared to answer similar kinds of questions. Favorite hard to answer questions are:

- What are your greatest strengths and liabilities?
- Give an example of how you can work under pressure.
- Why should we hire you for this job?
- How can you make a contribution to this company?
- What are your two or three greatest accomplishments?
- What interests you about this job?
- What interests you about this company?
- Why are you looking for a job in this field?

As you can see, these types of questions are thought provoking. *Be prepared!*

THE SELECTION INTERVIEW

If you're invited back more than twice, then you're on the last lap. The selection interview is the final hurdle in getting hired. All candidates have submitted an application or résumé, while many were tossed aside at first glance. There was the screening interview, where basic questions were asked and your responses were noted. Factual matters, or your type of answers could have influenced the results. More applicants fell by the wayside at this point, so if you were invited in again, it probably means you are one of the final contestants. And the winner, at this stage, will get the job-offer.

In a selection interview, an hour or more may be taken to reassess the information needed to form a final hiring decision. Generally, many of the same kinds of questions will be repeated from previous interviews, but the main purpose here is to determine whether or not you are the kind of person who will "fit in." Sometimes, because of the supervisory levels involved or the expertise involved, a department head or a specialist in your own area may have discussions with you.

A NOTE ON REJECTION

Being rejected is not necessarily detrimental. Sure, it can be depressing, but you can't know all the company's reasons for making choices or exclusions. They can differ markedly from your own evaluations. If you turn the rejection against yourself, you unnecessarily erode your self-esteem. *Strength* is the thing that, somewhere along the line, will pull you out of the thundering herd of competition, and give you the opportunity you seek.

Part II

Breaking into
the Media Professions

Chapter 6

NOTES ON BREAKING IN

Now that you know how to launch yourself into the media, let's look at the professions individually, so you have a good idea of how and where you can, and want, to fit into the business—how best to channel your energies, job-hunting efforts, and the presentation of yourself.

It should be obvious to you by now, that *if you really want to break into any of the mass-communication fields, no entry-level position is too menial for you to take.* For once in the slot, you have the ability to make much more of it—to learn about the field and the other opportunities within the company for which you will be qualified (once you have a little experience under your belt).

Why are there more jobs these days for insurance underwriters, practical nurses, and public accountants than there are for junior account executives, production associates, and copy boys/girls? There is no doubt that the media professions are all very enticing. Indeed, they've earned a worldwide reputation as the "glamour" professions (although there is much hard work, and frankly, little that is glamorous). Perhaps a better way of phrasing it would be to say that they are *challenging, exciting,* and offer you an *opportunity for growth* far beyond what other businesses can offer.

To assist you in your job search, it is important to know more about what each of the businesses is *really* like—beyond the career guidance manuals, the government leaflets, and the brochures you find in libraries or receive from trade associations and professional societies.

What you need to know is the view from the inside, from people who are involved with the profession on an everyday basis in the fields of publishing, advertising, public relations, broadcasting and film. It's important to hear from (and you will) the people who are working, now, in their first entry-level jobs. Through them, you learn how they got their job, what it's like on a day-to-day basis, and what they see as the path to moving up. You'll also hear from people who have already moved up from entry level, to positions with more responsibility and more of a chance to learn the nuances of the business. Their comments should give you insight to the ways you can create opportunities for yourself, and also provide you with a better perspective on the industry. Finally, you'll hear from senior people in each field who have made it, not so much to find out how they got into the business, but to find out what they look for in the young people they hire, what they have to say about the opportunities in the media industries, and how you can use that information to help you break into the field.

Breaking into the media professions is not an easy thing to do. Indeed, the purpose of the first part of this book has been to educate you to the fact that it takes a lot of planning and effort on your part to get that break. However, the important thing to remember is that *it is possible.* What's more, you don't have to be the smartest in your class, or the one with the most work experience (although, admittedly, it helps) to get a job. There is no single, foolproof method of breaking into the media professions, just as there is no one sure path to the top rung of the corporate ladder. *If one way doesn't work for you, try another.*

THE HURDLES BETWEEN YOU AND YOUR FIRST MEDIA JOB

Although job opportunities and starting salaries have generally been on the increase for recent college graduates, according to estimates issued by the College Placement Council, there is a "no gains" prediction for the communications industry in the early 1980s. Of the twenty-eight professions considered, only the education and government fields will fare worse than that of communications. But predictions for the later eighties look a bit more positive, according to a recent survey by the New York *Times*. In the Communications section of the survey report, it states: "Two trends signal heady times for communications-related industries. One is the public's growing hunger for information—to make decisions as consumers, to gain influence in their jobs, for self-improvement and entertainment. The other is technological, the emergence of new outlets for information, such as cable television and teletext, that have filled in the traditional gaps between the print and broadcast media." And thus, the economics of "supply and demand" come into play.

If you want to break into the media professions, *you must be prepared for the fact that your starting salary will probably be far below what you feel you justifiably deserve* (and you're probably right!). Competition for entry-level positions is extremely stiff and this partially accounts for the low-level income. The other factor is you just don't have the practical experience that comes from on-the-job training. So, be prepared for a salary range that is "grotesque" (as one media executive phrased it). If you can deal with the fact that your income level will be minimal, and instead can look at the job as an opportunity to learn, then this apprenticeship will be a lot more meaningful to you and financially more palatable.

In addition to stiff competition, many training programs have been eliminated from corporate budgets as businesses look for more and more ways to "tighten up" their balance sheets. Years ago, there were many "trainee" positions available for aspiring young people with talent (and/or "contacts"), but money has been tight for more than a decade, and so these positions have become tight, too.

In some of the media professions—especially radio, television and film production, and to some degree, newspapers—unions may be the reason you have trouble getting a job, keeping one, or initially getting the work you really want to do. In these fields, many of the key jobs (reporter, talk-show host, cameraperson, director, writer, etc.) are unionized and unions can have a dramatic effect on your ability to get a job. For example, unions can set the limits on the number of people hired, their salary, length of employment, type of work they can and cannot be asked to do, and who can or cannot be used to substitute for them. If you are in the union and have a good contract, the job security and the well-defined limits to your job can be a comfort. However, if you are not in a union, can't get a job you want unless you *are* in a union, but can't join a union because its quota is filled with people who show no signs of quitting or who are years away from retirement, it can be a frustrating situation.

Finally, you might come to blame automation for cutting you off at the pass, particularly if you have your heart set on a career like the editorial side of newspapers. One of the traditional entry-level spots in the newsroom has always been copy boy/girl—those are the young people who fly around the office, grabbing sheets of copy from frantically typing reporters, and rush them to the waiting hands of the editors. But this is the 1980s and the era of the video display terminal, the new electronic typewriter that offers a reporter a computerized screen, instead of a sheet of paper, on which to compose his or her story.

"In theory, the job of copy boy shouldn't exist anymore," remarked one former copy boy. "But paper still exists, and someone has to move it. Besides, reporters will always want someone around to get coffee!"

THE JOB SITUATION IN MEDIA

In spite of the problems of tight money, union quotas, and space-age technology that cut into the opportunities available to recent college graduates, the fact is that there are still jobs. Thomas W. Moore, a former president of ABC TV Network, who now heads Tomorrow Entertainment, a film production company, had some words of encouragement: "In media, there's been a steady and complete acceleration over the last fifty years. Radio has grown tremendously. And commercial television—well, it only began in 1948. And the point of this is that the acceleration of the media will continue, and along with it, an acceleration in the number of jobs available. There will be more of a need for creative people and more employment in all facets of the business. The whole industry is changing and growing. Now there's cable (paid television) and all its factions. There's all sorts of subsidiary rights activity going on (books sold to Hollywood and novelizations of films are two key examples of "subsidiary rights"). Each decade brings a greater need for bright, responsible and talented people entering the field. Because of this, we've got to take our chances on the younger ones trying to enter the field."

He continues, "In broadcasting, the major markets are the younger ones, under forty. So in motion pictures and radio and TV, there is a lot of money to be made for people under forty. Young people have a better opportunity to sell themselves because they are part of the very market broadcast is going after."

GETTING IN AND GETTING TO THE TOP

Although there is no single, foolproof way either of breaking into the media professions or of threading your way to the top, there are some fairly predictable ways of getting in (contacts, campus recruiting, mail campaigns, personnel agencies), and there also are the traditional routes to the executive suite (sales manager to book company president, junior copywriter to creative director, copy boy to city editor). But once you are in the business, you will realize that media people often approach their careers with as much spontaneous creativity as they approach their work (even on the administrative end). They skip stages in the traditional corporate structure or change from creative roles to business functions and then back again; they switch from magazines to books, newspapers to P.R., advertising agencies to clients of them. And the best part of this somewhat unpredictable career tracking, is that *it is a perfectly acceptable method to get ahead.*

Thomas Moore has some words of wisdom on that subject too. "At some point in all media, you've got to make up your mind in which direction you're going—creative or business. But when you're breaking into the communications field that doesn't mean you should turn down production because you want creative, or vice versa. As a matter of fact, very often you will go from business to creative, or the reverse. That's what I did—and I think it gives you a better perspective—and that's what a number of people who have risen high up in the business have done.

"Broadcast and film offer a unique opportunity to rise high because, unlike most corporations where there is a structured hierarchal pyramid with a broad base, the industry hasn't matured yet and the pyramid hasn't reached its pinnacle. In fact, right now, the pyramid is nearly in reverse—difficult to gain entry, but almost boundless opportunity once you break in."

The same is true of advertising and public relations, which are also relatively new industries (advertising dates from the post Civil War period; public relations from the early part of this century), and even the publishing business, which has evolved over centuries, is currently in a state of change and expansion that is resulting in previously insignificant areas, becoming "action central."

Still, and because they can be helpful, the following chapters include typical organization charts for the media professions. These charts will give you an idea of what jobs naturally follow from the entry-level positions you may be offered.

A WORD ABOUT DEAD-END JOBS

New people in the media professions occasionally find themselves dead-ending, in spite of their best intentions. One woman, now writing promotional copy for a hair-care products company, is planning to use that job as a springboard to a beauty editor's slot. This is her fifth job in the five years since she graduated from college. Each job had initially looked to her like a good entrée for a media dream career, but none of them were, and it seems, in each case, it was for a very good reason.

The first job she took was at a major woman's magazine (perfect, right?). But the job she took (and she admits she really just fell into it), was as the assistant to the renewal promotion manager in the circulation department. As you'll see in the chapter on publishing, circulation responsibilities are on the business end of magazines and, in fact, have nothing to do with the writing or editorial side; hence, it can be a dead-end job for an aspiring writer or editor (though it could be the golden opportunity for a budding publisher).

Next, this woman obtained a job at Time-Life as a photo-lab assistant. This time, at least she was in the creative end, but quickly found out that what she was doing was far better training for making a career in the art department end of publishing. So then, she took a job at one of the "Big Three" television networks. First, she was assigned a plum position as the assistant to the production supervisor for an afternoon soap opera—a great job, but only for someone wanting a career in television or film production, not for a person wanting a career in journalism. So the woman changed jobs in the company to a desk assistant's job in the newsroom, thinking that it would be a stepping stone to writing, but it proved to be nothing more than a secretarial position.

This is not a happy story, but it does prove a point. *It pays to find out about the job before you take it*—to know whether it really is a spring-board to what you think you eventually want to do, or just another job that needs doing in a big corporation. This is not to say that this woman was unwise to take any of these jobs, but the choices were unfortunate, because her expectations were substantially different from what the opportunities offered. If she had gone into any of those jobs knowing *what* to expect, she could have put in her time, used the position as an opportunity to grow, learn, *and* produce, and at the same time, have sought job openings within the corporation that could have led her more accurately on her career path. She had expected each job to automatically lead her into writing, and so when they didn't, she left. She saw them as dead-end jobs (and they were for her career path of writing), but left each company and the other possible opportunities within them. And, had she been more aware of career tracking, she could have looked for and chosen another job, before accepting any of these in the first place.

EDUCATION AND TRAINING

Chances are, if you now have an interest in getting into any of the media professions, your college transcripts reflect that inclination, in terms of your choice of major or minor studies, in the courses you took to fill various academic or credit requirements, or just to fill time gaps, in your class schedule. English majors abound in the media professions, particularly in the creative jobs, as do art, journalism, communication, film and radio-TV majors. Also prevalent are people with liberal arts degrees in subjects such as anthropology, religion, and political science, who took every writing or art course he or she could or was a disc jockey for the local radio station or an editor of the school paper. On the creative side, advanced degrees and specialized training can be helpful to certain companies and jobs, but generally speaking, they are not essential. On the business side, however, and particularly in advertising, an advanced degree is becoming increasingly important. Said Peyton Sise, Manager of Advertising for Avon Products, Inc., "In marketing, nothing short of an MBA is particularly helpful."

Sarah Staten, formerly Director of Special Sales for a major publisher of art and photography books, agrees. "Arriving on the scene with an MBA puts you in terrifically good stead and pushes you up a number of notches before you even start."

Jane Wolchonok, Marketing Manager at Citibank, agrees with Sarah. "I worked for more than three years in the consumer products division of a medium-sized company without my MBA. I was taking courses at night, but then I decided I would really go for my degree fast—on a full-time basis. Eighteen months later, I got a job at Citibank—I wanted to go with a big company with a good reputation. My feeling was that you could always go from big to small, but it's a lot harder to go from little to big. Anyway, I don't regret having taken the time off to get my MBA. In fact, I think it was exactly what I needed. It was the answer to everything for me. It gave me confidence. It opened doors. Now I know the lingo, the terminology and how to use it. Proportionally, I am advancing at a much more rapid pace."

Ed Cooperman, Vice-President and Marketing Director, Gold Card, Division of American Express, who regularly recruits for his company, put it this way, "I prefer MBAs. They have a deeper background, a greater depth of knowledge in finance and marketing. Particularly on the client side, but on the agency side, too, since agency people have to implement a (marketing) plan—which is often very technical and "numbers" oriented. Another thing, I find that people with a general liberal arts background usually spend more time on the job searching for what interests them most. MBAs either like it or they don't. They often seem to know better what they want."

Nowhere is it written in stone, however, that you have to complete all of your training before you get your first job in a media profession (nor that you had to have majored in the field in college!). Each year, thousands of college graduates take entry-level jobs that enable them to see how a particular business or company works and also pay them enough money to both live and attend night-school courses taught by working media professionals. It's not the easiest way to get through the heavy course load to earn an MBA, or the demands of other courses necessary to enhance your career path (*although it's done all the time*), but it can be the best way to learn the specifics you need to know about advertising, copywriting, art, television production, public relations, or copyediting techniques. As Peter Kerr, a young hopeful at the New York *Times,* explains, "In fields that are less structured or defined—like the media—you've got to enter the community (the newspaper community, advertising community), to get an idea of what's happening, how it's done, what's involved."

WHAT ABOUT NEW YORK CITY?

There is no question that New York City is the capital, the mecca, the Big Time of most of the media professions (although for broadcasting and film, so is Los Angeles). Every national magazine, with the exception of *Playboy* and *National*

Geographic, is published in New York. Nearly all of the major American advertising and public relations agencies are head-quartered, or have offices, in New York (although they are no longer all on Madison Avenue). The three major commercial television networks, ABC, CBS, and NBC are all head-quartered within a six-block stretch of the Avenue of the Americas and, with only a few exceptions, most of the large book publishing houses (as well as many of the smaller ones), are found in New York.

This certainly does not mean, however, that you can't have a media career if you live in another part of the country. Many times, it even *helps* to get started out of town, and you can. Although the range of opportunities is more limited, an out-of-town career can be every bit as rewarding, successful, and lucrative as one carved in the highly charged, supercompetitive, and superexpensive, number one market of New York City. "New York pretends to be the navel of the world," says Bo Niles, Home and Food Editor of *Mademoiselle,* "but I really don't think there's any such thing as provincialism anymore."

Also, it is a known fact that in the newspaper and broadcasting businesses, if you have your eye on a coveted glamour job in New York—your own "beat" or specialty as a reporter for the New York *Daily News,* as a television anchorman/woman, or radio disc jockey—you may *have* to get yourself out of town for a while. "Make Philadelphia stand up and take notice," is the way Michella Williams, an editor of the New York *Times Magazine,* puts it. "People really should know that there are plenty of good places to start in Chicago, or Boston, or Cleveland—places like that, they have *good* papers, well-respected papers. I look around at the people that are being hired here and they're all from other cities. I came to New York—although that's a few years ago now but, really, if you go for the big time immediately, you're often beat down by the time you're twenty-seven."

WHAT ABOUT THE GLAMOUR?

What are the media professions really like? Is public relations a life of three-hour lunches, gray flannel suits, and fast trips to the Coast? Or is it long hours, boring meetings, and lunch at your desk? Is advertising a world of designer furniture, blue jeans in the office, and a social life sparked by the presence of models, film directors, and commercials shot on location? Or is it endless revisions, cantankerous clients, and gunmetal-gray filing cabinets?

Likewise, how literary is the environment of a book publishing house that needs best sellers? How hilarious are television comedy scripts that *must* be ready to go by the end of the week? Or how glamorous is it for *Today* show hostess, Jane Pauley, to arrive at the NBC studios each morning by 6 A.M.?

"Other people find my job glamorous and exciting. Absolutely!" said one P.R. executive. "Not only do they perceive it as exciting, but also—mistakenly—as so-called easy work. They think that doing publicity and public relations for a prestige company means sitting behind a large desk in a wonderful office. They see me on the phone talking to the press, batting my eyelashes and never dirtying my nails. That's *very* far from the way it is."

Looking at book publishing, Jared Kieling, Senior Editor at Arbor House, talks about the glamour of his field: "There's a tweedy image, a notion of tradition and gentlemanly publishing, which is increasingly less valid, especially within the new areas of opportunity in the book business. It was said to me once by a paperback editor who had just returned from England that just as his fellow paperback editors are becoming increasingly like West Coast movie people (!), hardcover editors are beginning to wheel and deal more like paperback editors, and the British are following along in the American tradition. That image of a quiet spot where literary talent is fostered is, I think, somewhat at odds with the frenetic and marketing-oriented atmosphere most entry-level people will encounter as editorial or sales or publicity assistants in busy offices. There is glamour, all right, but the kind of glamour is changing."

More to the point, particularly about the entry level, is this comment from a publishing executive: "Oh, it definitely has its glamour side. But the glamour isn't what pays you good money and you don't get promoted on glamour. Publishing can provide you with very comfortable environs, with nice people, intelligent people, so that you forget you're starving and can't pay the rent."

So, the honest answer to the question, "Are the media professions glamorous?," has to be "yes"—and "no." During the early years of your career, you can expect to experience plenty of the long hours, low pay, endless revisions (or rejections), and other unglamorous aspects of the business. You may find yourself running for coffee, typing until your fingers cramp or, as one would-be New York reporter did for six months, moving your boss's car every time alternate side of the street parking periods expire! But, yes, there are "goodies" later on . . . Senior media people do take long lunch hours (to conduct business more often than not, or as one magazine editor put it, "The higher you go, the less frivolous your lunches become") and advertising and P.R. agency offices do tend to be well-furnished with wall-to-wall carpeting, smoked-glass conference tables, real wood desks and lots of fresh flowers and greenery. And yes, "creative types" do occasionally wear blue jeans—*designer* blue jeans—to the office, but as far as models, film directors, big-name authors, and television stars are concerned, some people in communications spend an entire career in the business and never, ever, meet a celebrity, while others end up marrying them. (A case in point is the now defunct marriage of advertising art director Stan Dragoti and supermodel Cheryl Tiegs.)

A self-described "new kid on the block" in broadcasting said, "Sure, it's glamorous. But that wears off. I mean, even he [and she points out a devilishly handsome and very popular newscaster]—even he doesn't thrill me anymore. You get *blasé*." And Parker Ransom, an account supervisor of Ogilvy & Mather Advertising, agrees. "Stereotypically, advertising is seen as glamorous, high-pressured, nonconventional and fun. But the 'glitter' is misleading. It's an intense business with a great deal of pressure, but it's more conventional than it is probably viewed by an outsider, having to match business, marketing, and statistical wits with a client. But," he adds, "it is a lot of fun."

"Is my job glamorous? Absolutely not! But it is challenging and intellectually stimulating, and at times, it's downright fun," says Heidi Bermacher, Advertising and Sales Promotion Manager for the Lodging and Transportation division of American Express. "I love my work. There's nothing else I'd rather do—it's a real opportunity. But what's glamorous about dragging oversized presentation books around the country or gobbling down a hotdog because you've got three minutes until boarding time or arriving home after four days on the road with a suitcase full of dirty laundry?"

If you're looking for constant glamour, you aren't going to find it in the media professions. But if you want challenge, creativity, and an opportunity to really utilize your potential, then you will probably find it. Besides, instead of glamour, you're likely to find that your career is *fun!*

DOING YOUR HOMEWORK

Finally, lest you think you can get off easily, each of the following chapters includes a section entitled "Doing Your Homework." You may feel that after four or more years of advanced education, the last thing you want to see is another reading list, and yet if *there is one thing the "old hands" in the media professions all agree upon, it is that they don't like to waste time talking to someone who knows nothing of their business.* Unfortunately, "homework" is as important and inescapable in the highly competitive job market as it was in college. Ed Cooperman of American Express says, "I want to talk to someone who has ideas. Even if they are wrong—at least it indicates a real desire on the part of an individual to produce."

Granted, no one who interviews you for an entry-level position expects you to know everything there is to know about a business. But then again, why blow your chances for a good job by drawing a blank if you are asked what you thought of Paley's book, or Ogilvy's, or Cerf's. In case no one else tells you, there are interviewers around—including some of the biggest big-shots in the media professions—who love to use aggressive, "trip-'em-up" interviewing techniques and will often try them out on young hopefuls, "to see what stuff you're made of." You can be ready for that sort of attack, or simply for a more productive discussion with a potential boss, if you've done some advance preparation in the form of research—reading and *thinking*.

Thomas Moore—and remember that he was *President* of ABC-TV Network—says it all: "I haven't sought to interview a break-inner for a job in a number of years, but sometimes some kid will write to me. And if the kid has done his homework— that is, if he knows about my company, and me, and knows what he wants to do, I'll be interested in him." He adds, "Much of what you'll be doing (homework) you can consider as early training for your career." He then asked, "Do you know how Fred Silverman got his job? He's the hottest name in TV right now. He got it by sending out his Master's Thesis, which was a reprogramming of ABC's programming for the six years prior to the time he did the thesis. And he sent it out with a cover letter to all the top people at ABC. It was a shock method and it was a long shot that wouldn't always work, but it worked for him. He told them that he felt they should have programmed the network the way he had. He told them if they did, it would raise their ratings and he showed them why. That got him a job."

Today Fred Silverman is a $1 million-a-year network television president. Enough said?

Chapter 7

PUBLISHING

In a broad sense, it is true that the book, magazine, and newspaper publishing businesses all exist for the same reason: to communicate news, ideas, and entertainment through the printed word, graphics, or both. Beyond this definition, however, the three branches of publishing are very different. For instance, a newspaper city room, with its "here today gone tomorrow" pace and focus on world events, bears more resemblance to a television newsroom than to a book publishing house; the business of publishing books, with its dependence upon direct sales to the consumer, has more in common with the emerging industry of *paid* television than with magazine publishing, which is in turn primarily supported by advertising.

The consistency of these professions, however, is the same. The people in publishing all share an interest in printed communication and the well-developed story—be it a work of fiction, a news item, or a nonfiction magazine article. Book, newspaper, and magazine publishing also share a common ancestry in the development of printing and distribution, and before that, the development of writing.

ROOTS OF PUBLISHING

Publishing is a very old form of communication (spanning over six thousand years!), which is still very much alive today because of its special characteristics that have transcended time. It is important for you to understand the roots of publishing, in order to put it into perspective with the other communication media and to see why publishing will be around for many years to come.

The origins of writing are from the fifth millennium, B.C., when the Egyptians "wrote" by carving hieroglyphics and the Babylonians etched cuneiforms in clay tablets. Naturally, reproduction of these written forms was not only a long, laborious process, but sharing the inscribed message was often physically impossible (i.e., moving a cave wall). Transporting more than one or two clay tablets at a time was extremely difficult, and so people began to look for a more workable way to communicate with written words and pictures.

The transition from writing on stone slabs to writing on paper came from the Chinese, who began writing on bamboo. But bamboo also proved to be fairly impractical, particularly when more than a few volumes were involved. Then the Egyptians developed a form of paper made from Papyrus, from which the word "paper" is derived.

The breakthrough that spawned the publishing industry occurred in fifteenth century Europe, when Gutenberg invented movable type. Though the establishment of printing presses was just one of the many cultural developments that took place during the Renaissance of Western civilization, those same presses played an important role in sustaining the effects of the Renaissance.

With this development in communication, a larger percentage of the populace became educated and informed, and could now communicate with each other and band together behind common ideals. Church and state viewed this development as a threat to their authority, since much of their power had been founded on the ignorance of the masses. This perceived threat resulted in censorship of printed material, a practice which has, fortunately, declined substantially over the years.

UNIQUENESS OF THE MEDIUM

Though all of the communication media make different demands on their audience, the products of the publishing field stand out as being the most demanding of effort. Unlike the products of broadcasting, books demand *active participation* from the audience—the physical act of reading—in order for there to be benefits experienced from the form. And because of this, the publishing business is based on the premise that the audience can read and indulges in the products of publishing—books, newspapers, and magazines—in a motivated way. The aim is to evoke a response from the audience, in thought or act. Because of the relative "slowness" between the medium and audience—single threads of information absorbed by readers at their own pace—there is considerable time for the reader to respond (develop thoughts and feelings) to the information being communicated.

As opposed to verbal communication and broadcasting, publishing is a "silent medium." The communication between readers and the printed word (unless read aloud) is absolutely silent. This silence is what makes the medium personalized and private in its communication, and allows room for introspection, analysis, and *re-examination* of the information presented.

In addition, because the information intake pace is completely controlled by the audience, publishing allows the audience to have a greater degree of freedom and power in approaching the medium. Unlike broadcasting, which often seems to be in perpetual motion whether the audience is involved or not, publishing invites the audience to participate in the exchange of information.

THE ROLE OF BOOK PUBLISHING IN MASS MEDIA

Although books, newspapers, and magazines have a common beginning in the form of the inscribed message, books provide a mobile permanence that magazines or newspapers cannot achieve. It has been said by some social historians that our civilization, as we know it today, could not survive without books. They are an essential part of the education process and are indispensable to the professional, business, and social levels of our culture. They are fundamental in measuring a civilization, and are an art form by which we can be judged.

Unlike newspapers and magazines, which convey the message of printed material within one to thirty days, books usually lack immediacy in their message, since even with the fastest production schedules, creating the publication takes a minimum of nine to eighteen months (and more than ten years in the case of Margaret Mitchell's *Gone With the Wind*). However, what books lack in immediacy, they make up for with good writing, editing, and production techniques.

Jared Kieling, Senior Editor at Arbor House, says, "As one might imagine, hardcover publishers think of themselves in terms of disseminating ideas of a fairly enduring nature, that warrant presentation in a book. And we think of ourselves as adding a certain emphasis, or importance if you will, to the works of worthy authors by investing in them and making a marketing effort to get them to the public. I think that although we may rarely reflect on it once we're in the business, subliminally there's a notion that one is involved in the culture, in the work of defining the culture."

Books, both hardcover and paperback, are a mass medium that discusses the economic, social, emotional, and political problems and opportunities of individuals, families, and cultures across generations and continents. (In fairness to magazines and newspapers, they also share in these objectives, but the historical perspective and depth of knowledge is what sets books apart from their companion media.)

This is a time of change for the publishing businesses, however, and although some of the changes are the same for each (increased competition, new emphasis on marketing and specialization, advanced printing technology), the focus of change is different in each case. A New York editor explains, "Traditionally, the way book publishing has been was that hardcover publishers would find, develop and publish new books, performing the functions of editorial guidance and the initial launch of a book with promotion and publicity and so forth, to make unknown authors a success and successful authors more successful. Then hardcover publishers would sell reprint rights to paperback houses—the income from which became increasingly important in the sixties. Now the shoe is somewhat on the other foot, with a lot of paperback houses buying all rights directly from the authors and in some cases either licensing the hardcover rights—backwards, as it were—to hardcover houses or simply publishing a book as an original paperback."

The Director of Special Sales for a major publisher of photo books elaborated on another way that publishing has changed in the last decade. "As the years have gone by and publishing houses knew it was going to be sink or swim unless profits were made, management began to look to other areas of publishing that could make money for their companies—namely subsidiary rights or what I eventually got into, special sales." She explains about special sales, "It's no more than a ten-year-old term in publishing that involves taking books into nontraditional markets—museum tie-ins, sales to television, putting gardening books into garden outlets—that type of thing. But now it's acknowledged from the minute a book is first considered that our department is instrumental in predicting the sales potential of a book. The same way they say, 'Oh, this is a book we should take on; there will be a good paperback sale,' they say, 'This is a book we should take on, there will be some great *special* sales.' "

THE ROLE OF MAGAZINE PUBLISHING IN MASS MEDIA

The magazine, as a form, combines both editorial and advertising as a means to educate, inform and entertain its readers. Unlike newspapers, which are frequently published on a daily basis, magazines are in a better position to interpret and analyze news and events with more accuracy and perspective. They are not published more frequently than once a week, and many publications appear biweekly, monthly, bimonthly, quarterly, and sometimes even annually.

Today, the trend in magazines is more specialized editorial content, whereas in the past, most magazines were primarily national in scope. Subsequently, the type of advertising messages in magazines were previously national in scope as well.

"The trend towards more specialized editorial started taking place in the sixties and early seventies," according to "Chip"

Block, publisher of *Games,* a specialty interest entertainment magazine. "The primary reason for the change came about with the development of television as a national medium," Chip continues. "It wasn't until the middle fifties that there were enough televisions nationwide to make a difference to advertisers—and then it was a whole different game. Advertising in general interest publications began to decline, and by the early seventies, the *Saturday Evening Post, Look,* and *Life* had all been laid to rest. These magazines simply could not compete with television. Television, you see, was cheaper, had more impact and greater immediacy than any of these broad, general interest magazines.

"At the same time, national advertisers began to look to target their advertising dollars. As a result, there was a real upsurge in both subject and regional special interest pubs.

"And if this isn't enough," Chip says, "it will probably all start to change again for several reasons. First, television has become expensive. Advertisers are beginning to recognize that the impact of TV is no longer as great as it once was. There is just too much 'clutter.' Second, with the advent of the videodisk and videocassette and cable, the television market is going to be a lot more fractured and is likely to develop much in the same manner as the magazine industry. All this means more growth and more change, and of course, lots more opportunity for those who wish to get into this field."

Basically, there are five different types of magazines to the consumer market: women's, women's/shelter, men's, special interest, and general interest. Each plays an independent role, with a sole purpose of disseminating news, entertaining, or informing, or any combination of the above.

There are changes occurring in the consumer magazine industry. For example, Pamela Fiori, Editor-in-Chief of *Travel & Leisure* says, "We're beyond the point on magazines where we can separate the visuals and the words, where we can be so wedded to the written word that we fail to see what's important to the reader. People expect pictures in magazines, so we've had to change our thinking—'No more 8000-word pieces, if you please,'" she teases. "We realized that we ended up saying nothing with all those words—and you can't get away with that anymore. You have to say something." She pauses and then adds, "We also can't get away with just publishing stories *we* like. A magazine has to have a consciousness, a guiding philosophy. An editor can impose a style, a viewpoint, but it's awfully important to understand to whom one is speaking. Statistically, psychographically—the audience is the key."

Most magazines are sold to the reader for less than they cost to produce, since it is the advertising revenues that publishers rely upon to support the publication and make it profitable.

In addition to the consumer market, there is also the business/professional market, with its plethora of magazines, newsletters and information services.

THE ROLE OF NEWSPAPER PUBLISHING IN MASS MEDIA

Newspapers are published weekly, semiweekly, or daily. The business of newspapers is fast-paced, high-pressured and always running to meet the deadlines for delivering the latest news to the public—in print and on time. The major purpose of newspapers is to inform the public with detailed, timely, and *objective* coverage of the news, and to influence readers with editorials and advertising. And where newspapers simply reported the news, even as recently as forty years ago, now they are expected to *report and interpret*—or evaluate—international, national, state, city, or just small-town events. Though newspapers vary widely in terms of staff, circulation, and scope, they always have similar physical make-ups, in that they all use newsprint, ink, and typeface.

You may wonder what the difference is between newspapers and weekly news magazines, especially since they seem to cover many of the same topics. The major aspect that separates these journalistic forms is perspective. Though they may be covering the exact same things that the newspapers have covered all week, the news magazines have more time to develop a sense of perspective. Though newspapers and magazines both report and interpret the news, magazines are in a much better position to research a new development, size up the situation, and then present a clearer, fuller picture to the audience. However, it is up to the newspapers to report the news quickly and without wasting minutes or words, state all the facts in easy-to-understand language.

The big change in the newspaper business is a technological adjustment. An increasing number of major newspapers have installed the new video display terminals in their city rooms and, as a result, have switched from "hot" type to "cold" type in the print shop. These computerized video systems can do everything from storing a reporter's copy to setting up a page. They are something like the reservations systems that have been in use by the airlines since the late 1960s. Just as an airline reservation agent can type your name, flight number, and telephone contact information into a permanent record that can be retrieved from any other computer in the system, so now a reporter can type his or her story into a memory bank and a copy editor can call it up on his or her own screen when he or she wants to check the punctuation or add a headline. Then, just as some airline computers also type out tickets, so now the production department of a newspaper can "set" and print a story by computer. "It takes some getting used to," is the reaction of one New York editor, "and you're really stuck when it goes down or jams. But, yeah, I like it."

WHO GETS THE JOBS IN PUBLISHING?

The publishing field, unlike the other media professions, evolved over many centuries and as a result, has "matured" the most (although certain aspects of it are very young indeed). This means that the physical structure of a publishing company is normally more in keeping with a typical organization, and the job responsibilities more defined than those in the newer media fields.

ABILITY AND TALENT

"For publishing in general, you should have a demonstrated ability to write decently—to put words together," says Cynthia Clark, Assistant Editor of *Print Collector's Newsletter*. "The language skills have got to be there; that's the first thing," adds

Steve Lawrence, consumer affairs Editor for the New York *Daily News,* "and you have to be able to take facts and make them lead to an idea, to what they mean."

In publishing, more than any other field, *you must have a true understanding—a love—of the written word.* Whether you're on the creative or administrative side of the business, you have got to understand and respect the power of the printed word. (And now, more than ever before, you've got to thoroughly understand the graphic end, too.)

"People coming into publishing are expected to be very quick studies, very sharp—able to take down a stream of instructions in detail and get it right, to make complicated phone calls, to get messages correct, to pay great attention to details—clerical details, editorial details. To go through contracts, charts, manuscripts and make small changes—that kind of thing," says a senior book editor. "So you need a very solid grasp of how to get things done, overlaid with being culturally with-it, and reading a lot. And being interested in—accessible to —new ideas, being comfortable with handling ideas."

KNOWLEDGE

Of the three areas of publishing, i.e., books, magazines, and newspapers, generally speaking, the latter requires the greatest specialized education. There are specific areas in any field which require a detailed knowledge of it, but in order to qualify for an entry-level position in newspaper publishing, you can almost count on needing a special line of study *before* you break in.

It's pretty tough to get a fast, overall grasp of what's going on if you don't understand the basics—and you've *got* to, because that is the very nature of the business. So, if you did not major in journalism, but think the newspaper profession is your calling, then start taking courses. And be sure to learn the technical aspects too.

And if you're highly motivated toward book or magazine publishing, but feel you need a better handle on the business, you might seriously consider the Radcliffe Publishing Procedures Course.

A recent graduate of the Radcliffe Publishing Procedures Course talked about this exceptional program for the book and magazine publishing businesses. "It's a real grind. Six weeks, six days a week, from nine in the morning to ten at night. Plus you still have to do homework. But people in the business know that if you've been through it that you're skilled, that you've broken your neck and spent that money—that you really want a job. And the people that teach are really big people in the publishing business, who come all the way to Boston to teach you. It's three weeks on magazines, three weeks on books, and they teach you EVERYTHING. You learn to edit copy, to index, to dummy up a magazine."

When asked who goes to the course and how to get into it, she explained, "Most of the people in it are recent college graduates. It's *very* competitive—they take only eighty people in the course. Some of them are there for the right reasons, some for the wrong reasons. The right reason is to learn to be skilled; the wrong reason is to get a job. But a lot of people go for *both* reasons and there's nothing wrong with that."

ATTITUDE

Getting a job goes a lot deeper than talent. Almost every executive interviewed for this book said that a positive attitude is prerequisite for getting the job. Alex Gotfryd, Vice-President and Art Director of Doubleday, had this to say: "Attitude is very important, especially at the entry level. Good manners and a cooperative spirit are essential and go a long way. You see, entry-level positions do not require much experience. Therefore, the person you wish to hire must be a talented individual. Still, talent in and of itself is not enough to succeed professionally. As an employer, you should sense that the applicant for a job is driven in a positive way, is willing to work hard and cares about doing well. I have interviewed exceptionally talented and bright people whom I wouldn't consider hiring because their attitude was so obviously negative and defensive and their enthusiasm for the job—virtually nil. I wouldn't want people like that working for me."

"I've had several assistants," says Marcia Vickery, Travel Editor of *Bride's* magazine, "and with each one it's been a slightly different job, because they were each good at doing different things. The assistant I remember best was straight out of college, but she was willing to do her very best all the time she was here and *that's* what counts. Enthusiasm means an awful lot because it gives you energy; it's contagious. And if the person you're working with has it, it can buoy you up even on days when you come in feeling lower than a toadstool."

MOTIVATION

When asked about motivation, publishing people also have some strong opinions. One editor remarked, "Most people today who are looking for a job have given some thought to the future or at least to why they want a particular job—and I'm generally turned off by the person who hasn't." To which another editor adds, "When we interviewed last year, I was really quite surprised at the lack of preparation by most candidates. Some didn't have a clue what the magazine stood for. What its editorial direction was. I think they expected that someone would help them along during the interview and ask *them* questions. They could have done more homework to read the masthead, to find out what different departments are covered, how many times a year the magazine is published, who advertises in it. There were all kinds of things they didn't know that made me think they weren't clear why they were there. That they just thought it would be fun to work for a magazine, but hadn't tried to figure out why they had come. A little bit of direction gets people a long way. And a lack of it gets them nowhere in my book."

WHERE ARE THE JOBS IN PUBLISHING?

Peter Kerr, who is just getting his career under way at the New York *Times*, explained that there are essentially five ways to get into the newspaper business: "Some just go out and get a first job as a reporter somewhere, usually in some smaller city. Or they volunteer someplace so they can learn. Then there are internships; a lot of papers still have those for the summer. Or you can lean on the experience you gained as the college paper editor to show the 'clips' (published stories) you've collected. Then there's Journalism School. But none of these ways is guaranteed."

Peter Kerr is right. None of them is guaranteed. In addition to the points he mentioned above, it takes perseverence and hard work to land that dream job. That's why knowing *how* to look for a job, *how* to sell yourself, and *where* to look is so important.

With the possible exception of a career in books, the publishing field has no geographic bounds. If you're seeking employment in the magazine or newspaper business, you can look for (and find) work just about anywhere. Every major city in the country has at least one well-known daily paper, not to mention the countless number of weeklies. Without exception, every area in the United States is served by some kind of newspaper. And with the changing editorial direction of magazines (as they position themselves more and more to the special interests and segments of the population) there are more opportunities around the country than ever before.

BOOKS

A Note on Book Publishing and New York City   If you're really interested in a career in book publishing, you may very well want to launch your career in New York City. This is not to say that fine book careers can't be made outside the New York area (it happens all the time), but when it comes to breaking in, it is often necessary to physically locate yourself where the greatest number of opportunities exist—and that's New York.

"Manhattan is the center of the publishing business," says an editor about the book business. "There are, of course, specialty and business book and religious book publishers all over the country. And, of course, there are Little, Brown and Houghton

Mifflin in Boston and Time-Life is now in Washington, but in the main, Manhattan is the place applicants are going to have to work if they want to get launched and stay mobile."

According to another editor, "Anyone who comes to New York and wants to enter publishing is likely to find it the same as I did. It's contacts, diligence, plodding and executive secretarial skills that eventually get you in—or possibly the Radcliffe Publishing Course. But you're still going to end up with the same job at the bottom of the totem pole."

Book Publishers   A vice-president of a major book publishing company gives this piece of advice: "Everyone wants to be an editor, to work with fabulous authors and great manuscripts. But I found that one gets a much more interested hearing if one goes in and says, 'I'm very interested in subsidiary rights.' That's the way I got started, working in the foreign rights department for a book publisher, which was a job selling translation rights to overseas publishers, mostly by correspondence— so it was a huge clerical load—but I also developed an ability to read contracts and to make deals and to appraise the commercial value of properties (manuscripts) and then put these selling points across. It's very shrewd to check out areas of a company which aren't besieged by people, to get into the company, know how things function internally.

"And then, if you work for someone or apprentice yourself to someone who is central and connected and busy and upwardly engaged in all aspects of the publishing house, then you'll see a lot, and learn a lot, and it won't matter what department you started in. If you can get a spot where you learn to read contracts and deal with them, you'll be in a good position to have clout and influence and stay mobile. Knowing how to read and interpret is essential in publishing if you want to get ahead."

Book Packagers   One of the least explored areas of publishing for job opportunities is book packaging. Essentially, a packager is to books as a producer is to the movie industry. It is the packager's responsibility to assemble the various elements of the book—the concept or idea, the research, writing, design, and editing—and actually deliver printed books. (Most people not directly involved with the book industry don't realize that publishers subcontract books through packagers.) Book packagers are important to the industry because they offer publishers the opportunity to buy a finished product without having to produce it all themselves.

"Books are produced outside the house for a number of reasons," says Jeffrey Feinman, President of Ventura Associates, a well-known and successful book packaging company, "sometimes because of the physical format of the book (it is not suited to the publisher's presses), but most often because publishers have neither the time nor the needed manpower to produce all the books they would like for their book list."

When asked how he got into the business (Jeff has been a packager for five years, and is in his mid-thirties), he had this to say: "Originally, I had an idea for a book that I wanted to write and I met an editor who liked the idea and bought it. Because I already had another established business in the sales promotion field, I was able to convince my editor that I should print the book, too.

"I wrote the book and produced it myself," Jeff continues, "and it did fairly well. The next time I saw my editor I had ideas for twenty-five more books. I soon realized that I could produce ideas for books much faster than I could write them. So then I looked for people who could write these books, and artists who could implement them and printers who could produce them.

"Book packaging is a great way to learn the business," Jeff says, "because it gives you the opportunity to learn more about the business in a hurry. At an entry-level position, you're likely to have to do everything from getting the coffee to sitting in on brainstorming sessions for book ideas, from researching at the library to approving press proofs on the book. You won't get that kind of initial exposure with a publisher, and with that kind of knowledge, it's easy to go places in publishing."

MAGAZINES AND NEWSPAPERS

As in book publishing, there are major growth areas in the magazine and newspaper businesses too. For example, as magazine production costs continue to escalate (and the subscription cost often can't keep up with this inflation), publishers look for new profit centers.

The publisher of a national monthly news magazine, has this to say: "A major growth area for some publications is to exploit their subscriber list—by selling subscribers other products and services beyond the magazine. This has been done, and very profitably, by offering books prepared especially by the publisher, newsletters, conferences, seminars, and special purchase opportunities and discounts on products advertised in the publication."

"A real growth area for women in magazine publishing," says Bernice Grossman, Circulation Director for *Co-ed* magazine, "is on the financial side. The editorial side is already loaded with women, but that's not true on the business side. If you have an MBA, you might seriously want to look into the opportunities that exist in business management. Especially with Affirmative Action, it's opened up many new areas, but there just aren't enough women who have had the special education (financial courses, MBA, etc.) to qualify. But believe me, publishers are looking for them.

"Another growth area," Bernice continues, "is in data systems and data processing (the computer end). Although there are a lot of highly qualified systems people working in publishing, there are few who know about *both* computers and publishing. For those who do, they can practically write their own ticket."

So, when you're looking to break in, consider doing some research on growth potential within the industry. Look for new areas of opportunity. Not only can you use this kind of job as a stepping stone into the mainstream of publishing, but often you can make the changeover with a competitive and prestigious edge, since you've had specialized training in a profitable area of the field.

Another specialized area, but far more traditional, is a career in art. About her own humble beginnings in the art department of *House & Garden* magazine, Carolyn Sollis, now an Assistant Editor, says, "I started on the very bottom level, labeling pictures, cutting out slides and photostats—doing the basics. Although it was not the slightest bit glamorous or intellectually stimulating, it was a good place to start for someone who wanted to move on. Yes, sort of a foot in the door. But, really, I think the art department was a good place to begin. I wasn't a typist and I really was in on the ground floor where everything happened. And I got an idea of our (*House & Garden's*) direction. What was a good photograph, what was a bad photograph, why something as simple as taking a picture of a room from this angle was better than that angle, a little bit about lighting, what photographers to use. Really, I felt it was the *best!*"

CAREER TRACKING IN PUBLISHING

From the point of view at entry level, the first question about career tracking in publishing may not be how far you can go, but how *low* on the totem pole do you have to go to get started, and how long will it take you to get anywhere. Anticipate that you will have to start at the very bottom in publishing. This means as either a secretary or an assistant—in either case, you'd better have some secretarial skills.

Secretarial skills, *especially typing,* are important in all of the media fields, but in *publishing, you will not even be considered for an entry-level position unless you can perform (at least partially) in some kind of secretarial function—especially typing.*

It is almost traditional to hire a very sharp and dedicated secretary to assist a publicity director, editor, director in sales or marketing, or some other senior person. In time, this secretary is given increasing responsibility and eventually, after a minimum of three to five years of training, will be promoted to some kind of associate position.

One other point to remember: Men are hired—just as often as women—for secretarial positions.

Books

About the editorial side of book publishing, one editor says, "There are plenty of women and men—you have lots of men as secretaries in publishing—who have gone that route and it has taken all of them the same time (roughly eight to ten years) to get to be an editor. I don't think you're going to make it sooner than ten years unless you get a very lucky break—if a top editor you work for leaves or dies and you take over the work or if you discover that unknown author who turns out to write a bestseller."

Notoriously, the book publishing field has a reputation for overworked personnel. If you're not willing to work incredibly hard and long hours and for low beginner's pay, you'll be unhappy in the business. One book publishing executive put it this way: "If you don't have a real desire to work like the dickens, it's very hard to be tapped for anything more exciting. But if you say, 'I'll write jacket copy, I'll write catalog copy, let me write sales letters on this book and write a report on it,' then it's very likely you'll become a valued employee and someone who is noticed in a business that is endemically understaffed and overworked."

Why is the tradition to start so low and wait so long? One publisher's reasoning on the subject makes sense: "It's possible to circumvent some of the entry-level stages, although most of the people in a hiring position had to come up that way, too, so it's usually difficult to convince these people that an Oxford education or an enduring love of books is more useful to them than being able to type eighty words a minute! The basic approach at the entry level should be to get a foot in the door in a position from which you can see things going on, to get in and do a bang-up job, killing yourself on weekends, working nights, and taking on projects, asking to be given projects outside of one's circumscribed area."

Patience is a quality highly revered in this business. If you go

Book Publishing

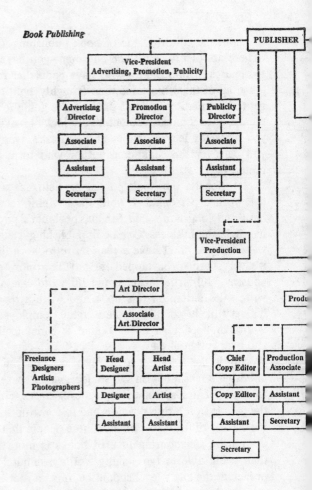

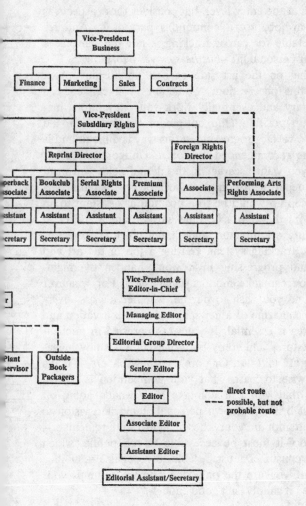

Vice-President Business

| Finance | Marketing | Sales | Contracts |

Vice-President Subsidiary Rights

Reprint Director

Foreign Rights Director

| perback ssociate | Bookclub Associate | Serial Rights Associate | Premium Associate | Associate | Performing Arts Rights Associate |

| ssistant | Assistant | Assistant | Assistant | Assistant | Assistant |

| ecretary | Secretary | Secretary | Secretary | Secretary | Secretary |

Vice-President & Editor-in-Chief

Managing Editor

Editorial Group Director

Senior Editor

r

| Plant ervisor | Outside Book Packagers |

Editor

——— direct route
- - - possible, but not probable route

Associate Editor

Assistant Editor

Editorial Assistant/Secretary

in expecting to move up quickly, to while away your hours in excitement and glamour, then you're setting yourself up for disappointment. This is not to say there won't be any excitement or glamour even at the entry level, but consider these aspects as moments in your job, not a continuous part of it. And remember, a timetable for career tracking is not the same as a timetable in your personal life—*business moves a lot slower*.

About tracking on the art side of book publishing, Alex Gotfryd offers this observation, "Sometimes you can enter a firm as a secretary and eventually work your way into a mechanical paste-up position (the bottom of the ladder in the design field). However, progressing in this way is difficult and is certainly not the recommended approach. Unlike many other professions, if you want a career in the design field, you must begin in an art department doing art work or art related activities. The next step up would be to a position as assistant to an art director. From there, you become an assistant art director yourself, associate art director, and finally chief art director. That's the basic tracking system. Getting a job in the art and design world and progressing in it won't happen overnight. Your preparation can take months, even years. For whatever aspect of the field you wish to pursue, whether it's an advertising agency, a magazine or a newspaper, keen observation and study of that area is essential. If you are interested in publishing, go to bookstores and study book jackets. Or study magazines—how they are laid out. Or pore over newspapers, if that's your aim. It's wise to learn what your competition is. Direct your talent so that you can compete with what's going on around you, but bring your own personal stamp and vision to anything you attempt in your chosen field. And remember—whatever you do—it must be accessible to the public, which means that the consumer must be able to recognize your idea for what it is. If you are the only one who understands your own project, then it simply isn't good enough."

Magazines and Newspapers

To get an idea of structure and possibilities for career tracking in magazine publishing, a reporter/researcher for a leading weekly news magazine, explains how the parent corporation and its magazines are set up. "The business and editorial sides are wholly separate operations, so I can't speak for the business side in any way. But the editorial side is composed of a triumvirate of separate departments; the writers, the news service, and the research staff. There's very little employee mobility among the three, in that it is extremely tough for a researcher to become a writer or a writer to join the news service. Writers generally become either Senior Writers or Senior Editors. Managerial types in the news service come from News Service, in Research from Research. Of course, rules are made to be broken and there are exceptions." He goes on to explain about the big jobs at the top of the ladder. "The head person of each of the individual magazines is called the Managing Editor, who is usually, but not always, selected from the body of managing editors. Incidentally, there have only been three Editors-in-Chief in the history of the company."

This journalist's comments illustrate that you can never pay enough attention to *where* your job will lead, and *how* long it might take you to get there. For example, if you were to take an entry-level position in any of those departments expecting that you could cross-over, you probably couldn't do it. But, if you took that same job with the clear understanding that it was a learning *and* growth experience, and that you might very well have to look elsewhere—after you had put in your time—then you could approach your career tracking quite differently, and probably, a lot more enthusiastically.

Steve Lawrence of the New York *Daily News* has this comment about how career tracking works in most newspapers: "I'm not sure there is a traditional track. It's so much determined by personality, who's comfortable with it. There are a lot of bright people who move up and then there are people who just stop at certain points, but the way it usually works is you go from reporter to City Editor—or National Desk or Foreign Desk—and then to the News Desk. News Desk is really the Managing Editor, who decides where a story will run in the paper, what the headline size will be. Then after that, it's Editor."

"I think it should be pointed out that not everybody wants to be editor-in-chief," remarks Marcia Vickery. "The salary may sound appealing (nobody *ever* makes enough money), but the editor-in-chief's job involves juggling everything from print orders and personnel changes to personal appearances and public relations, and that may not be what you're good at. So you may very well choose to stay on a lower rung of the ladder where the kind of things you do day-to-day in your job are fun and exciting and pleasant for you. I think growing in a job is as important as achieving a higher job level. How well you do and how far you go depends on what you are willing to put into the job. And I don't necessarily mean overtime hours. It depends upon the *quality* of work you're committed to turning out when you *are* working. On a given day, it may be only three hours—at a conference away from the office—but if those three hours are top-quality hours, they're going to move you. People are very willing to help you along as long as you're sincerely interested." She then added, "Years ago a number of young people who came into beginning-level jobs seemed to believe all they needed to do was sit there and type sporadically until the inevitable moment when the editor for whom they were working stepped in front of a fast taxi, whereupon—Zap!—they would become instant editors. But it didn't work that way then, and it doesn't now."

BREAKING INTO PUBLISHING: A VIEW FROM THE INSIDE

BOOKS

Jennifer Brown is a 24-year-old Assistant to the Editor at one of the largest publishing houses in New York. Having started as a secretary to the Editor-in-Chief two years ago, she now looks ahead to the time when she'll move from Assistant to the Editor to Editorial Assistant, a distinction that means the difference between doing secretarial duties while learning the editorial process, and working only in an editorial capacity, with the status of a "junior" editor.

"When I was the secretary to the Editor-in-Chief, he had an

editorial assistant, so I was largely confined to administration-related tasks such as typing memos, letters and reports, filing, and other general office duties. While editorial secretaries and assistants do perform those same basic functions, their work directly relates to editorial projects. The material I worked on related, essentially, to how the editorial *groups* functioned. The bad thing about that was that it got pretty boring, since individual books interested me more than how departments ran. But, despite the tedium involved, it was good for me because I rapidly learned how the company worked. I also learned a key lesson: *never let a piece of mail cross your desk without understanding it.* If your job includes opening and sorting the mail, make the most of it. It's incredible how much you can learn by really reading the office mail, rather than just passing it along.

"Another fortunate thing—probably the best thing about the job—was that my boss was more than eager to teach. If I didn't understand something, all I had to do was ask. He was a wonderful person to work for in that way. Naturally, you do have to pay your dues, and I paid mine. The phone drove me crazy sometimes—it was not unusual for all four office lines to be tied up—and if that didn't get to me, going for coffee, xeroxing, and the pile of unsolicited manuscripts did.

"After a year I made up my mind that I wanted to go into editorial. With the approval of my boss, I made it known around the company that I was looking. The personnel department posts job openings as standard procedure, but if you're lucky, as I was, you'll hear about a job the same day someone has 'given notice,' so you can express interest right away. After interviewing, I got my present job working for a senior editor."

When asked about her average day, Jennifer said, "I try to get in before nine. How eager to learn you are can be indicated by your willingness to come in early and to stay after five. Besides, in my case, that's practically the only time I can see my boss during the day. That's also when most editorial work goes on—before nine and after five.

"For a business that is so slow in producing the product, a book—it can take anywhere from nine months to, in one case here, twelve years—it's hard to believe how fast the pace is during office hours. The phone is constantly ringing—it can be an author, an agent, the art, production, publicity, sales or business department, or it could be a seven-year-old kid wanting to know how to get in touch with Mark Twain. The mail is non-stop—there is always some kind of problem to be dealt with—and things always must be done NOW. There are packages to be sent out or picked up by messengers, manuscripts waiting to be rejected, and more. And while these routine things are going on, my boss must get to a meeting, or has someone waiting to see her, or has a special project to do for *her* boss. It never stops and there is *never* nothing to do. Actually, there's always too much to do, with no end in sight.

"So why do I do it? It's not the money, I assure you. The basic thing is that we're all here because we love books. Not just to read or to look at, but to participate in their creation—everything from the words to the binding to the jacket. It's amazing. You have every different kind of person working here, yet, because we all have the bond of books, we can relate to one another very easily.

"A special aspect of this job is the relationship between the editor and assistant. I'm an apprentice. My boss is teaching me how to be an editor. When I'm ready to do more work, independently from her, that's when I can expect to be promoted, if an opening comes up, to editorial assistant.

"In editorial there are a lot of us 'apprenticing.' Every editor has a secretary or assistant, and every one of them is just as determined, and as devoted to books as the next person. The trouble is that editorial assistant jobs—the next move up for all of us—are very few in number, and the turnover rate for each seems to be about two years. In editorial, it can be a long wait for promotions on our level, no matter how good you are."

Magazines

The career of Richard Story, now a Senior Editor of *Travel & Leisure* magazine, is proof that a mail campaign to get a job is not a waste of time; he did it twice.

"I was going to go to law school, but then I began to realize that that was what I *should* do, it wasn't what really interested me. But I knew I had to get a job. I'm from Oklahoma and it was either get a job or go back, and I knew I didn't want to do that. So I used the career counseling service at school (he went to Williams College), because I figured that was a good place to start. I didn't know what I wanted to do and I had this amorphous idea about publishing. I knew I wasn't into hard news, so I wrote off newspapers right away. Book publishing I didn't really know much about, but I did know I liked magazines. I'm the kind of guy who needs his "magazine fix." I'll go out on a Monday morning and spend $15 on magazines. So I put together a file of all the Williams graduates who were in magazines and I wrote to all of them, out of the blue. And one guy was a V.P. at *Reader's Digest*. He called me about three weeks later and said he wanted me to see some people there. So I saw three or four people and got the job. Funny part of the story was that the guy—the V.P.—had never gone to Williams! He stopped by my office, maybe six months after I started, and it turned out there wasn't even anybody in his family who had gone there."

When asked about that first job, Richard continues, "I was a fact-checker. That's one of those traditional entry-level jobs you find at the big old established magazine places—like *Time, New Yorker,* that were all started about the same time in the twenties or thirties; they do things that way. But, really, I think fact-checking is one of the best entry-level jobs you can get. You avoid all the secretarial duties, you get to work with the editors and with the material. And it's different than in book publishing, where you can get into copy editing and get stuck. In fact, a lot of big magazine editors started as fact-checkers at Time-Life, places like that. Anyway, I stayed at the *Digest* two years and then decided it was time to leave. So, back to the mail campaign. I used *Writer's Market* to get names (see Doing Your Homework in Publishing, page 154) and just sent out cold letters to all sorts of magazines. Nice, straightforward letters. And I got two calls from that; one from a guy who used to be managing editor here (*Travel & Leisure*) who said he didn't have anything at the moment, but wanted me to come in, and one from an airline that publishes its own in-flight magazine. I took the job at the airline, but it turned out to be a total disaster, so I stayed only two months. *But,* it did establish me as an editor, so that I went back to *Travel & Leisure* and this time there was a spot as an Associate Editor. That was two years ago, and I was just made Senior Editor this fall. Down the road, sure, I'd like to be an editor and maybe move over to a more general, life-style type of magazine.

"By the way, do you know what Helen Gurley Brown (Editor of *Cosmopolitan* magazine) does? She asks everyone who comes to work for her if they read the magazine, and I think that's really important. You've got to think about what sort of magazine do *I* read? What do I read *about?* You've got to know what interests *you* and then go for that."

NEWSPAPERS

Peter Kerr, twenty-three and a recent graduate of the Columbia School of Journalism, was promoted after six months from copy boy to clerk assigned to the Metropolitan Desk of the New York *Times.* Although he sometimes feels like "a perennial entry-level person" (he writes stories only occasionally and only during his free time), Peter chose to accept a job of low rank and responsibility to be with a "top flight paper" when he might have gone to Trenton, New Jersey, to become a "star" by now. He tells why:

"I had a plan outlined early on. From the time I was eighteen, I knew I wanted to be a journalist—a reporter. That I wanted to get into a good grad school and then get a good paper and eventually be a foreign correspondent. Then, after I got into Columbia, I knew that if I wanted to get a *good* job after I graduated, I had to do something outstanding. You have to do a kind of thesis there—maybe sixty pages—so I decided to do mine on deinstitutionalized mental patients. And what I decided to do was to *live* in a home for released mental patients. So I went in in some bedraggled clothes under a false identity— all that. Well, there was a *lot* of stuff going on there, so I talked to one of my professors at Columbia—who's with the *Daily*

News—and she called the paper and we ended up doing the story together, with a split by-line. It ended up in state hearings, the whole thing. But as a result, I had a really good record when I got out of Columbia. You know, the plus that no one else had."

He thinks a moment, "You know, that's what I'd tell anybody who wants to get into the newspapers. Do whatever is required and then more. You have to do *more*. I think that's what is necessary to get a good job—going one step beyond what is required."

He continues, "But I'd tried for about six months to get a copy boy job at the *Times*, but they really hire very few and even then only one in ten makes it. But I kept writing to them. Then I decided to do a try-out at the Trenton *Times*. That's something a lot of papers do; they bring you in as a reporter for a set amount of time and they let you do stories and see how you fare. Most places give you a week or a couple of weeks. In Trenton, they gave me two days! So I worked for forty-eight hours without stopping—I did a couple of stories actually—and I got an offer from them. In fact, I was all set to buy a car, to get an apartment down there, the whole thing. A lot of my professors were saying, too, 'Take it. Even if you get the *Times*, go to Trenton.' Then I got a call from the *Times* to come in for an interview, and even with that, my professors were still saying, 'Go to Trenton.' But I met a friend of mine on the street, who had started at the *Times* as a copy boy and has done pretty well (he mentions a recent block-buster story the friend had covered) and he said, 'Come on up to the newsroom.' Well, I saw that place, with all those desks and—I mean it—I began to salivate. And over in the corner there was this guy, Syd Schanberg, who won the Pulitzer for his reporting in Cambodia, and I know *he* started as a copy boy there. Well, my friend asked me if I wanted to meet him (Schanberg) and I said, 'Sure.' And I ended up telling Schanberg about the Trenton thing and he just looked at me and said, 'I don't like to give advice. Either route could work. But, I know I don't read the Trenton *Times* that much.'"

Magazine/Newspaper Publishing

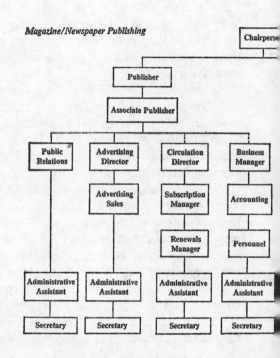

——— direct route
— — — possible, but not probable route

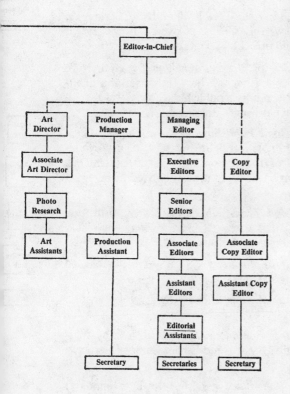

DOING YOUR HOMEWORK IN PUBLISHING

ADVANCE READING

Publishers on Publishing, ed. by Gerald Gross (Bowker, 1961): Essays that cover various aspects of the book publishing business.

A History of American Publishing by Charles A. Madison (McGraw-Hill, 1966): Covers all the major companies, past and present, in context.

The Art & Science of Book Publishing by Herbert S. Bailey, Jr. (Harper & Row, 1970): "Editorial and financial operations of a modern publishing house" by the director of Princeton University Press.

The Business of Book Publishing by Clive Bingley (Pergammon Press, 1972): Straightforward category-by-category delineation of the responsibilities and parameters, including subsidiary rights, contracts, and editorial work on a manuscript.

The American Book Trade Directory, Twenty-fifth Ed., ed. by Jacques Cattell Press (R. R. Bowker; biennial): Lists all the publishers, book clubs, etc.

Ayer Directory of Publications (N. W. Ayer; published annually): Lists by state and category.

Ulrich's International Periodicals Directory (R. R. Bowker; annual)

Introduction to Mass Communications, Fifth Ed., by Warren K. Agee, Phillip H. Ault, and Edwin Emery (Harper & Row, 1979)

The Literary Market Place (R. R. Bowker; annual): *Writer's Market:* Describes magazine and newspaper editorial formats and gives details of the types of books handled by publishing houses.

LEGENDS OF THE BUSINESS BY LEGENDS OF THE BUSINESS

Editor to Author: The Letters of Maxwell E. Perkins,

New Ed., ed. by Maxwell E. Perkins (Scribner's, 1979):
Letters to his authors by one of the greatest editors of
American publishing history, including Thomas Wolfe,
F. Scott Fitzgerald, and Hemingway.

Paris Was Yesterday by Janet Flanner (Popular Library,
1973): About authors, artists, publishing and the *New
Yorker* magazine, by its long-time Paris correspondent.

At Random: The Reminiscences of Bennett Cerf by Bennett Cerf (Random House, 1977): Stories of his career by
the publishing executive who became a personality in the
early days of television.

AFTER YOU GET THE JOB

Book People: Self Portraits by Burt Britton (Random
House, 1976): Once you know a few names and faces in
the business, this is an amusing compendium of self-
caricatures.

A Dictionary of Modern English Usage by Henry W.
Fowler, ed. by Ernest Gowers (Oxford University Press,
1965): The "Bible."

The Manual of Style, revised Twelfth Ed. (Chicago University Press, 1969): The "prayer book."

The Elements of Style, Third Ed., by William S. Strunk,
Jr. & E. B. White (Macmillan, 1978): The "hymnal."

KEY TRADE PUBLICATIONS

Publishers Weekly ($45 per year; R. R. Bowker Co.,
1180 Avenue of the Americas, New York, NY 10036):
Almost exclusively for the book business.

Folio Magazine ($36 per year; Folio Magazine Publishing
Corp., P.O. Box 697, 125 Elm Street, New Canaan, CT
06840)

B.P. Report ($65 per year; Knowledge Industry Publica-
tions, Inc., 2 Corporate Park Drive, White Plains, NY
10604): Exclusively for the book business.

Chapter 8

ADVERTISING

WHAT IS IT ALL ABOUT?

Advertising is the business that produces the ads and the strategies that sell the products and services of American and foreign industry; it also is often the business that dreams up new products in the first place, or that will be given the task of pumping new life into ailing and forgotten products when ordinary salesmen and old-fashioned selling techniques (or bad advertising) have failed. It is an imaginative business that utilizes any number of solid concepts of psychology and group dynamics (among them greed, competitiveness, narcissism, recognition/identification) and it is also a business that is firmly based in the principles of economics and statistics. In short, advertising is a selling business—with a capital "S" for sophistication.

Although advertising employs the techniques of graphics, it is not art. Although it depends upon good writing, it is not literature. And although it utilizes the most sophisticated methods of modern marketing, it is not Big Business (even the largest advertising agency is a relatively simple structural operation by comparison to the fiscal and managerial complexity of, say, Xerox or General Motors). This is not to discourage artists, writers and MBAs; it is meant, however, to point out a reality of the business. Sure, there are creative awards to be won that carry as much prestige, maybe more, than Hollywood's Oscars, and account executives do get to engineer heavy-duty, big-money new product launches that can change the dynamics of the national economy (imagine working on the introduction of

Coca-Cola or McDonald's?). But—and this is the essential challenge for anyone interested in advertising—you're not there to write poetry or living drama, to art direct minimovies or to postulate impressive economic concepts. You go into advertising to sell products and services, to create ads, commercials, and marketing strategies that will justify a client spending thousands of dollars per *second* to buy a "slot" in prime time TV (8–10 P.M., the so-called "family viewing period").

The scope within that essential boundary, however, is vast. And vast and imaginative solutions are the lifeblood of advertising. People in the business still talk, for example, about an ad that was done in the late 1960s that provides a good example of both creativity and salesmanship. The ad for Volkswagen ran full-page in newspapers and it simply said, "Think small." Like most good ads it sounds a bit flat just to state what it said, but "Think small" as the single line of copy, underlying a small, centered profile of a Volkswagen, is what is called a concept. And until you can either create concepts or figure out how to make them work strategically, you won't go anywhere in advertising.

Explaining to someone who has never been in an agency, what a concept is and how it works is a major task. A concept can be the thematic foundation of your advertising—the basic idea upon which your entire ad campaign is built. It may be expressed through the marriage of words and graphic elements, ordinary when standing separately, but thoroughly impactful when used in combination. If you add to these definitions that the reason for creating a combined idea is *to communicate a succinct and solid sales message,* then you have an idea of what good advertising is all about.

Test the concept of the VW ad by asking three questions: What does the picture mean without the words? What do the words mean without the picture? And finally, what do the two together *really* say about a Volkswagen and why to buy one? By fleshing out the total visual, textual, and subliminal message of the VW ad, you should get this message: The next time you buy a car, why don't you *think* about buying a *small* car—one that will be easier to maneuver than the big car you now drive, that will fit into smaller parking places, that will cost less to buy, that will use less gas per mile, and, if you reach for other implications, perhaps a car that was designed for the "little guy" in our society.

WHO GETS THE JOBS IN ADVERTISING?

The people who get the jobs—the good jobs—in advertising are the people who understand how to create and use concepts. It's as simple as that. "You have to be able to look at a bar of Ivory soap and know what to say or to put down visually to make people want to buy it," says Binnie Held of Barbara Stevens Associates, an executive search firm (commonly known in the business as "head hunters"), where Binnie principally recruits writers and art directors. "I know the thing that's looked for the most is the quality of the thinking, the ability to turn a little trick in the head and make something come alive. It's not just putting together words; it's putting them together in a new way. Or laying out a page with visual excitement."

She's right, although the ability to successfully visualize and conceptualize comes with practice. That's why *it is so important to read print ads, direct mail, sales promotion, to listen to radio commercials, and watch what's on TV. It all goes to give you a feel for what's happening in the business.*

Beyond that, if you have creative talent, you must put it to use, even without a job. Jack Stern, head of his own New York-based art studio, has this advice: "Do some speculative pieces for local businesses and offer them for a price—however modest. If they get used, you'll have a professional sample. If they don't, you'll still have something you did for a particular client."

A vice-president of a New York advertising agency screens both creative and account people on all levels, including the entry level. He says about creative people, "Beyond entry level, you look for qualifications—qualifications in the book, the portfolio" (yes, you have to try to create a few ads if you want to get your first creative job). "Then you look for something special in their make-up, some singularity of personality, originality of thought and expression. You don't look for blind conformity, but you need to see some signs of discipline so you don't get some curly-headed kid who can't conform at all."

Asked about account executives and entry-level people on the account side, he says, "The one qualification is brightness; it leaps out of a successful candidate. A kind of smart intelligence, or intelligent smartness. Coupled with what I call reasoned assertiveness and common sense, which really is the key to business sense. Knowing that an agency is a profit-making institution, that paperclips cost money, too. We're also looking for careerists, not just people who want a job so they can ski a lot. You know, the old work ethic has dissipated. Today, people want to live well-rounded lives, and there's nothing wrong with that, but you've got to have enough commitment to your work to be dedicated and involved."

Unless you have been to art school, you might not understand the real competitive edge that a portfolio can give to the person seeking creative work. Jack Stern has this to add: "I might see a person without a portfolio as a professional courtesy, but I would not necessarily consider that person for a job. The portfolio tells me a lot beyond just what their creative talent is. Is the portfolio presented in an esthetically pleasing way? Does it contain just a few outstanding pieces or is it also packed with a lot of junk? When I'm hiring, I'm looking for someone who can take over some of the mechanical work and I'm looking for quality. If a person gives me a sloppy book, with no attention paid to pieces selected, I pretty much figure that's the way they are on the job."

Portfolios are considered essential if you want to get a job on the art side, but they are also important if you want to write. So, if your schooling did not include making up a portfolio, then you should consider taking a course that will help you to do so.

Ed Cooperman, Vice-President and Marketing Director for the Gold Card Division of American Express Company, agrees: "I look for people who are bright, who are doers. And I like high-key people who get nervous and excited, who make the product part of their life."

WHERE ARE THE JOBS IN ADVERTISING?

In the old days—and the 1960s constitute the old days in advertising—there were formal training programs at many of the big agencies in New York and other major cities. Most of these were geared to careers on the account side of the business (a few agencies also offered copy competitions, however). Young men (it *was* the sixties, not the seventies) were hired in groups of ten to twenty to spend six months to a year rotating through various departments; two months in media, one month in traffic, a week in the library; it varied from agency to agency. That kind of formalized training is now an on-again, off-again thing. More often than not, it is directly tied to the amount of business an agency has and the need for entry-level personnel.

A recent survey, "Occupational Outlooks," presented by the New York *Times,* states, "The 180,000 advertising-related jobs, heavily concentrated in New York, Chicago and Los Angeles, are expected to rise faster than the average for all occupations in the next few years. The growing variety of consumer goods, and the increasing self-awareness of specific consumer markets —women, minorities, the old, the young—will be contributing factors."

Where, then, can you get a good start? If you want to break into advertising, it is very important that you have a good feel for what area appeals to you in the business. Although advertising is a more loosely structured business, in many ways it has more "dead end" jobs than those in the other fields. For example, media, which can be an exciting specialty in advertising, is just that, a specialty. "The ladder up," according to Tim Sharpe, General Manager of McCann-Erickson Direct Response, a division of the agency, McCann-Erickson, "usually does not include lateral moves. If you start in media, you're likely to stay in media."

"The overall role of media, while important, is not crucial to the agency," Tim Sharpe, who is also a Senior Vice-President of the general agency, continues. "No account has ever switched agencies because of a great media department."

"The way media tracks," says Tim, "is that you would start at the trainee/intern level, then progress from there to assistant buyer, buyer, group supervisor, and finally media director. The reason media usually doesn't allow for lateral moves is that it is such a segmented department. Let's say you start in media and you've worked hard and you're finally promoted to media buyer. It's not the broad job you think it might be. Even within buying, it's very segmented. You'll be the buyer for network television, or spot TV, or outdoor, or transit. But not for all of them. As a supervisor, obviously, you have to know about all media, but you can see just how segmented this area is."

"If you start in media," according to Tim, "be sure that is where you want to stay, or else be prepared to take a lateral move out of there as soon as you have any experience (within a year)." Otherwise, you're likely to find it a specialty in which you must stay, or make a downward move from at some later date.

There are exceptions to every rule, and there are a number of media superstars who do much more than direct their agency's media department. Herbert Maneloveg, a Senior Vice-President at Della Femina Travisano & Partners, Inc., is one. Not only is he a specialist in media, but he is a real generalist as well and an integral part of the agency's new business team. Eugene De Witt of McCann-Erickson is also considered another media superstar whose abilities go far beyond the media department.

Creative and account servicing are still considered the two biggest areas in advertising, and most paths to the top lead from one of the two.

For creative spots, Binnie Held advises that many of the major opportunities are at the big agencies. "They're growing bigger and bigger and buying each other up or buying up smaller places—all over the country and even overseas—and they're *always* looking for people. Plus, they deal with clients who have more money to spend, so that it's the kind of thing that if you can creatively conceive it, there will probably be the money to execute it.

"But really, the thing I'd like to say to anyone breaking in is to stay away from the fly-by-nights. Now I don't mean the small, quality 'boutique' type of agency, where there can be a lot more opportunities and you can move up fairly quickly—but I've had people come in here telling me about their paychecks bouncing." When asked how to determine the difference between agencies, she went on, "Call around and find out what kind of reputation they have, if you've got suspicions. And check them in the Red Book (see Doing Your Homework, p. 170). Look at the number of employees and the billings and how they're handled. A good clue is to look at the names and the titles. If you see that the President is Joe Smith and the Secretary-Treasurer is Sally Smith and the Creative Director is Harvey Smith, then you have a pretty good idea you're dealing with an agency where it's going to be difficult to move up unless you're part of the Smith family."

To out-of-towners, she advises, "Still look for the major agencies, Ogilvy & Mather, J. Walter Thompson, McCann-Erickson—they're all over the country now. And look for places with national products—not just local—so that the work you do will be of significance when you want to come to New York five years down the road. Or even if you never come here, you still use the same criteria about what you work on. And one more thing, while you're working, never stop working on your 'book.' Constantly re-do it. It's never finished, it's not a static thing." When asked what entry-level jobs to go for and which to avoid, she added: "I don't think it's a problem for a writer to take a copy typist job, but it is a lot more difficult for an art director to get out of the 'bullpen' (the studio where ads are put together). It's better to get something as an assistant to an art director. Having a mentor is extremely important. You'll do rendering and things like that, but you'll be assisting one person and that's important. They teach you things."

Ideally, it would be wonderful to start off in an entry-level position as an assistant to an art director, but most newcomers won't have this break.

"If you have no art training," says John Marinello, Vice-President of The Graphic Experience, a New York-based multimedia advertising agency, "then you have to start from scratch. Go to school to get the background. But most kids don't realize that even with top-level schooling, that the salary level will be 'grotesque.' I started in the business thirteen years ago making $60 a week and I was lucky to get that. You have to look at your early years on the job as an apprenticeship. You've got no experience and now you've got to get it.

"Art School teaches students to be creative, but it just doesn't teach them the realities of the business," John Marinello continues. "You can't be discouraged too easily. Most of the kids I see today have a lot of talent, but when they don't get the job, they take it personally—like they aren't any good. Also, plenty of times they have their sights set too high for the entry-level position. They think that because they have all this schooling and talent that they should start off as an assistant art director.

"My advice," says John, "when you get out of school, is to make a decision as to which way you want to go. To the bullpen at an advertising agency or to a studio (which is a lot like the bullpen, but it is not part of an agency—it is an art studio to which work is subcontracted by agencies). My personal opinion is to stay out of the bullpen unless you're going to be working for a top agency like Doyle, Dane & Bernbach. At a studio, you generally learn more, because, unlike the bullpen, which is just involved with the creative, you get to learn about everything, from tissues, through mechanical implementation—even printing. And if you've had experience at a studio, you shouldn't have any difficulty making the transition over to an agency, since you have been deeply involved with their business."

WHERE CAN YOU GO IN ADVERTISING?

Advertising is a fairly simple business, as far as corporate structure is concerned. Discounting the usual support system of personnel, accounting, mailroom, etc., there are only two main career paths you can follow in any agency, large or small; Account Services and Creative Services. (And if you have no interest, talent, or training in writing, graphics or print and film production, you may want to forget Creative, or at least be

prepared for a longer learning time in the beginning stages of
your career.)

Account services is the side of the business that deals
directly, and most often, with the client (i.e., the corporation
that has a product to sell), keeps track of deadlines and who is
doing what and when, and makes sense of all the facts and figures and significance for future campaigns.

In servicing the account, each product or group of related
products is handled by an account group, whose number is determined largely by the account's "billing" (that's the amount
of money spent for advertising each year). Usually an account
group consists of—from top to bottom—a management supervisor, an account supervisor (these roles are sometimes combined in smaller agencies or on small accounts), an account executive (or executives), an assistant account executive (or two
or three), and account assistants (or secretaries). Plus, each account group is augmented, when necessary, by representatives
of the allied departments of market research and media.

To explain market research, it is the department that obtains
demographics, psychographics, and other information (who
lives where, earns how much money, and buys what), evaluates
the facts and figures on magazines, newspapers, and broadcast
programming and media (which women read *Cosmopolitan*
and how many people watch "60 Minutes," etc.).

Traffic is also on the account side, which essentially is a cler-
ical-type department that plays in-house messenger during the
preparation of advertising and keeps track of all the myriad
production details.

Creative, on the other hand, deals with the product to be
sold, develops the selling "concept" ("Things go better with
Coke" or "The Marlboro Man") and "produces" the advertising.

On the Creative side, divisions of responsibility are also
made on the basis of accounts (products or groups of products), although the overall structure and working relationship
of the department is generally less predictable than account
services. At the top, generally, there is a Creative Director who
oversees everyone and everything; below the Creative Director,

there are two parallel ladders, one of art directors and another of copywriters. On the rungs of these ladders, working down from the top, are supervisors and group heads, senior art directors and senior copywriters, art directors and copywriters, assistant art directors and junior copywriters and, at the bottom of the heap, art assistants and copy trainees (the last two job categories are generally found only in larger agencies and may also involve semisecretarial duties or, on the art side, "paste-up" work). All along these ladders writers and art directors are "teamed" on various accounts; generally, two people with the same level of experience are put together, but not always; also, a writer or art director may be teamed with different partners on different accounts.

Somewhat more simple is the structure of allied departments under the general heading of creative services, print production, and broadcast production. The first is the department that orders type, processes photography or illustrations, makes the "mechanicals" (the "originals" of an ad) and orders "proofs" (the reprints of the finished ads, which are sent to the publications). Similarly, broadcast production handles casting of the "talent" (actors or voices) for the commercials, collects "bids" (estimates) from radio and film production "houses" (companies), keeps track of expenses for each separate commercial, organizes the "shoot" (the filming) or the recording session, oversees "postproduction" (editing and mixing, which covers the selection of tape to be used in the final commercial and the addition of special effects), orders "dupes" (the films or tapes, in quantity), and "ships for air date" (sends completed commercials—film or tape—to the networks for broadcast).

Remembering that the shortest distance between two points is a straight line, take a look at the following chart and you will quickly see which jobs and departments could be spring-boards for what you eventually want to do. You'll also see which are potential dead-ends and where lateral (and occasionally, retrograde) moves make sense.

Advertising

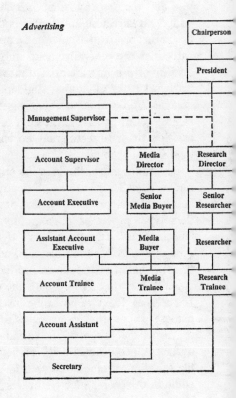

Account Services

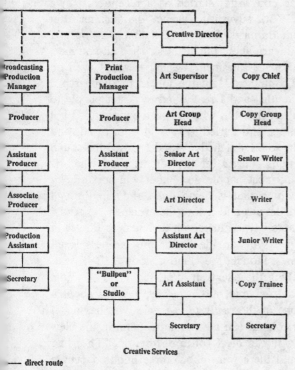

Creative Services

—— direct route
- — possible, but not probable route

BREAKING INTO ADVERTISING: A VIEW FROM THE INSIDE

At twenty-one, "the baby" of a Chicago advertising office is already a junior copywriter; it happened for her primarily because she knew what she wanted to do and never missed an opportunity to learn. "It's great," she says about her job, "and I get to work on everything my boss works on."

This rising young copywriter started as a receptionist at a medium-sized New York advertising agency the summer after her graduation from Barnard College. "But that was lousy. I mean, *what* can you learn about the business when all you meet are messengers and space salesmen? Really! I wasn't even on the *executive* floor. But then I got the job as the copy typist after a couple of months—and I really had to pester people to get that job, let me tell *you*—but when I was a copy typist I got to know *all* the writers, and I tried to look at a lot of ads and know what was going on. I watched TV and I turned the sound *down* for the programs and *up* for the commercials, which is the *opposite* of what most people do. But if you sort of *glut* yourself with everything that is being done and flip through magazines and read the ads and ignore the articles . . . And I used to ask the writers I typed for about the changes I'd see in their copy. That gives you an idea what the business is all about, too. Sometimes, though, they kind of took their frustration out on *me,* calling the client an idiot, that kind of thing. But I tried to learn from that, too. Anyway, I heard about a copy competition one of the *really big* agencies was having—it was in Dougherty's column (an advertising column in the New York *Times*)—and you can *bet* I got in on that one! They had me do some ads—and there were about three hundred people who entered and then they picked about twelve or fifteen finalists. And I was a finalist but I did not get the job." Anyway, I was on vacation in Chicago, where my mother lives, and just on a whim I took my portfolio with all that contest-entry stuff and talked my head off to some people and got a job. The pace is slower in Chicago; you get more attention there. And

people think you're *credible* because you come from New York
—just because you've even *lived* there. Even though I hadn't
been a writer in New York, they *knew* I was like semijunior,
trying, and in the competition. The main thing, though, the way
to know what you're doing, the way to get your *head* into it—is
not only to look at all the TV and print you can, but to be in
the *presence* of writers and art directors. Watch what they do
and see *how* they do the work. And talk to them, pester them,
and just be around. Then, if you *hang out* with them, you can
know what goes on; otherwise, you're sort of far away from it
all. Every so often I see a book of someone who's never been *in*
an agency or near an agency and they've been sort of a *student*
of all the commercials on TV. And they bring in things that are
impractical because they don't know how to do it. Or they pick
TV situations which are unfeasible and inaccurate for what a
camera can do. Or they write print that doesn't make sense and
—like, it's a pun and you don't know why." She laughs, "But I
did some of those, too. *Tons!* Many, many potato ads that were
not ads—you didn't know *what* they were!"

Asked about her work day, she continues, "It's very good
there. There are four creative groups in the agency and I'm in
one that has about fifteen or sixteen people and there are various teams. I work with a senior art director who is about thirty-
five and this is really good, and then we are partners with an
executive copy director—she's been in the business *forever*—and
her partner's an executive art director, a mild-mannered guy—
he worked on a major cigarette account. And what we do
sometimes is we lock ourselves in a room without a phone and
come up with concept statements. It's really fun because we all
give input. Just now we had a big *crunch,* and we each wrote a
commercial. Like, we did it all together, but we each brought in
a germ of an idea. It's very helpful to me; I can learn a lot from
them. But, also, I'm *allowed* to talk, to try whatever I think
makes sense. I often learn that something is *stupid,* and I edit
myself before I speak or show people ideas. Anyway, we each
wrote a commercial and the creative guy—the big guy—he chose
my commercial. You know, I'm given a *chance.* I'm never not
busy. And like I said, I work on everything my boss works on."

DOING YOUR HOMEWORK IN ADVERTISING

Get set for some good reading, and a lot of it. More than for any of the other media professions, there is a wealth of good books about advertising, including a couple of real winners in a category that is best labeled: "Legends of the Business by Legends of the Business":

ADVANCE READING

Reality in Advertising by Rosser Reeves (Alfred A. Knopf, New York, 1961): One of the classics that will always be timely. Explains USP (the Unique Selling Proposition) and the guts of the business in a fairly small book.

Truth in Advertising and Other Heresies by Walter Weir (McGraw-Hill, New York, 1963): A fairly sober book; soft-spoken and scholarly; but some insights are to be gained from Weir's pursuit of his ideals in the arena.

The Aberrant Image of Advertising (pamphlet) by Conrad Hill (University of Nebraska Press, Lincoln, Neb., 1960): Heavy-going and negative about the business, but balances the gung-ho points of view.

The Crazy World of Advertising (play) by Simon Hopkinson (Australian Theatre Workshop, 1975): Four "productions" that show how a campaign is put together; the character notes in the beginning provide some whimsical, and accurate, descriptions of different jobs in advertising.

John Caples: ADMAN by Gordon White (Crain Books, 1978): A member of the Copywriters Hall of Fame, Caples began his advertising career over fifty years ago; a great overview.

How to Put Your Book Together and Get a Job in Advertising by Maxine Paetro (Executive Communications, 1979): A creative manager (in charge of screening applicants for copy and art jobs) answers the most frequently asked questions and provides tips (from pros) on "how to put your book together and . . ."

Standard Directory of Advertising Agencies ("The Red Book") (National Register Publication Co.): Look here for names of agencies and lists of the clients they handle.

LEGENDS OF THE BUSINESS BY LEGENDS OF THE BUSINESS

Blood, Brains and Beer: An Autobiography by David Ogilvy (Atheneum, New York, 1978): An autobiography by one of advertising's titans, who wrote his first ad when he was thirty-nine; not a long book, but it brings you into contact with many other advertising "legends" and includes "11 Lessons Learned on Madison Avenue," one of which is, "The consumer is not a moron, she is your wife. Try not to insult her intelligence."

Giants, Pigmies and Other Advertising People by Draper Daniels (Crain Books, 1974): Glib, but intelligent, portrayals of people and "moments" in advertising, with sound comments on the business learned over thirty years; an example, "Advertising is a relatively simple business, made difficult by complicated people."

From Those Wonderful Folks Who Gave You Pearl Harbor by Jerry Della Femina, ed. by Charles Sopkin (Simon & Schuster, New York, 1970): Subtitled "frontline dispatches from the advertising war," this provides more stories of the "biz," and the big names in it, by one of the great copywriters.

George, Be Careful by George Lois, with Bill Pitts (Saturday Review Press, New York, 1972): Subtitled "A Greek florist's kid in the roughhouse world of advertising," this book includes many outrageous tales of the business and the personalities who continue to dominate the creative side; terrific insights, too, into what are good concepts (Lois is one of the all-time great art directors).

AFTER YOU GET THE JOB

Confessions of an Advertising Man, by David Ogilvy (Atheneum, New York, 1963): Ogilvy is perhaps the most universally revered giant of the business and this is perhaps the most universally revered "bible" of advertising; as no-nonsense and hence powerful as the man who wrote it, and as the ads that made him famous, chapters include: How to Get Clients, How to Keep Clients, How to Build Great Campaigns, How to Write Potent Copy, and How to Rise to the Top of the Tree—Advice to the Young.

Ayer Glossary of Advertising and Related Terms (Ayer Press, New York, 1977): Basic and useful; the title tells all.

How to Advertise by Ken Roman and Jane Maas (St. Martin's Press, New York, 1977): Presented as "a professional guide for the advertiser" and "for students of advertising"; includes brief descriptions of each area of operations and offers sound information on such topics as positioning, concepts, testing of ideas, legalities; in his foreword to this book, David Ogilvy (the long-term boss of the authors) said, "When you have read it, you will know what it took me 25 years to learn."

Advertising Pure and Simple by Hank Seiden (AMA-COM, New York, 1978): Written by a man known to enjoy helping young people get started in the business; includes five chapters on how *not* to do things.

The Best Thing on TV—Commercials by Jonathan Price (Penguin, New York, 1978): Basically a review of the successful (i.e., memorable, well-produced, best conceived, most sales generating) commercials; benefits any student of film, television and broadcasting.

KEY TRADE PUBLICATIONS

ADWEEK (incorporating ANNY) ($30 per year; A/S/M Communications, 230 Park Avenue, New York, NY 10017)

Advertising Age ($40 per year; Crain Communications, 740 Rush Street, Chicago, IL 60611)

Art Direction ($14 per year; Advertising Trade Publications, 10 East 39th Street, New York, NY 10016)

Backstage ($32 per year; Backstage Publishing, Inc., 165 West 46th Street, New York, NY 10036): Including weekly section on television commercial production.

Chapter 9

PUBLIC RELATIONS

WHAT IS IT ALL ABOUT?

Just as most people think that all there is to advertising is creating glorious four-color ads for glossy magazine pages and producing dynamite television commercials to sell a client's products or services, most beginners think that public relations is simply a matter of finding a million ways other than advertising to keep a client's name in the news, in the editorial pages, and on the air, without paying for space or time.

If you're familiar with the business at all, you are aware that every time you read in a trade publication or newspaper that John or Jane Executive was promoted from assistant sales manager to sales manager, or that XYZ Computer Company has developed a new product or reported increased earnings in the fourth quarter, most likely the public relations department or agency has sent out the news.

Every time you see an author on a talk show or hear a speech by the head of a big organization, chances are that a P.R. person has been involved in "selling" the author or the speaker, writing the speech and/or coaching the speaker, and making the necessary travel arrangements. But that kind of highly visible public activity is really only *publicity* and publicity is just one tool of the public relations practitioner.

Then what is public relations? P.R. takes on many different forms and titles, depending on the corporation or the organization. In fact, at one time there were several hundred definitions! Most were so confusing and so misleading that the Public

Relations Society of America has come up with a few that would be valid. One goes as follows:

> The public relations profession in servicing the legitimate interests of clients or employees is dedicated fundamentally to the goals of better mutual understanding and cooperation among the diverse groups, institutions and elements of modern society.

As you can see, this definition allows a great deal of flexibility within the profession as it relates to "public relations."

Probably the most important thing to understand is that public relations is a matter of two-way communication. It is telling the organization's story to its publics (and there can be many of these, i.e., consumers, the business community, the government or employees), and helping to shape the organization and its performance by feeding back information from these publics, which tell management what is expected of it. In short, public relations starts with an organization's policy and is definitely a management function.

But there are a lot of entry-level jobs you can start your career with in that highly visible area—publicity. In addition to preparing news releases and servicing the press, these jobs can include such pleasant events as sponsoring a "Visit to Santa Claus" party for underprivileged children, events which result in positive news coverage or material, or fielding tough questions from the media when your company has been accused of polluting a nearby river. (Not all news is good news, remember.)

This brings us to a very important difference between advertising and public relations. While it is the joy of public relations people to keep a client's name in the news to create a favorable or necessary impression, simply getting the company's name in the newspaper is not always enough . . . and sometimes it is too much if the impression isn't what you want it to be. Advertising *buys* the space or time it needs to present a message it wants, but publicity must accomplish the same basic end—a favorable image for the client—without spending one penny for editorial coverage and without control over the final story.

In seeking publicity, a corporate P.R. person or an account executive in a public relations agency must persuade a newspaper (magazine, television or radio station) that the client or the client's product is *so* important, interesting and/or newsworthy, that it should be featured in editorial (i.e., the nonpaid "news" or human interest portion) of the publication or broadcast schedule. That requires a sense of news and timing, as well as persistence and persuasive ability. Diplomacy too is needed, when it is the press that initiates the contact and asks for a "statement."

There is another difference between advertising and the publicity function of public relations. In advertising, you may promote a product (such as an automobile) or a service (an airline's service to London, for example). In public relations, you also may promote a car (in the business press as well as to the automotive editors), or an airline's services (by arranging a press trip for journalists on the first flight aboard a new aircraft), but in addition, you may be promoting the corporation that produced the product (in trade publications and financial and business news pages, or by involving the corporation in special promotions and industry activities).

Your client may be a person (an author, a rock star, a politician, or a business person), an institution (a college, a symphony orchestra, or the local zoo), an organization or association (a trade union, a foreign government tourist office), a special project (Save the Whales, Vote Proposition 13) or an event (Olympics 1984, Israel Fashion Week). In fact, the client can be almost any individual or organization that wants visibility, or needs advice on reaching its publics and has the money to pay a P.R. person's salary or the fees charged by an agency.

The fun of P.R. is that you become involved in doing many different things; and the means employed to build good will or to get publicity can be as creative and varied as the imaginations of the P.R. people involved. The problem in the area of publicity is that there is no way to guarantee results to a client. The only successful publicity effort (or publicist), therefore, is the one that gets results, and results are determined by two things: 1) The *quantity* of news "generated" on a client's behalf and, more important perhaps, 2) the *quality* of that news, in terms of presenting the client as he wants to be presented (or in the image you have advised the client is in his best interests).

The pinnacle of a publicist's success, then, is to have the news release "picked up" (that's when the written "story" you submit is used by a publication or broadcaster). If the media then call for more information, or if your story is picked up by a wire service—with the result that it may appear across the country or around the world—then you really have achieved results. Similarly, getting a client on "The Tonight Show" or the Donahue talk show can be a "coup," as is writing a speech for a college president that is then quoted in the newspapers, or dreaming up an idea like the Budweiser Clydesdale Horses. It's all part of public relations and it's all fun for people who are suited to it.

WHO GETS THE JOBS IN PUBLIC RELATIONS?

After twenty-six years in the business, Richard Weiner, President of Richard Weiner, Inc., a public relations agency in New York, and the author of six books for P.R. professionals (see Doing Your Homework in Public Relations, page 190), has a clear view of what he considers essential qualities for a successful career in P.R.: "If you think that getting along well with people or being verbal and articulate gives you ability in P.R., you're naive. It certainly helps to verbalize well, but the bulk of what everyone in P.R. does is 'trivial.' In other words, you have to pay attention to detail; you must appreciate this detail work and not be frustrated by it. And *you must know how to write*. Absolutely. In the 1980s more than ever you will have to know how to write in this business, and I am talking about *precise* writing. There's a tendency for the naive beginner to say, 'I'm an English major; I can do that.' But P.R. is journalism, and writing is still the basic skill."

Richard Weiner continues, "You need a lot of self-confidence, too. And optimism. Public relations has a low success ratio vis-à-vis advertising and that's hard for a beginner; they feel rejected. Plus, there's always this crisis atmosphere in

P.R., this catch-up mentality. You have it in advertising, too; it's probably the nature of a service business, which both are. But a lot of personality studies have been done about P.R. people and they say that the most successful have harnessed their neuroses to cope with these crises." He stopped to clarify, "Now, that's not to say we're neurotic. I think it's dentists that have the highest suicide rate—but there are frustrations in this business, so you've got to be well-adjusted, stable, square. And enthusiastic. Even the people in the business with inside jobs have to have enthusiasm. And curiosity; curiosity is very important. Because you have to be forever studying and learning and putting ideas together. That's what all media people do; they put together what they've read or seen or heard in other places. That's why I always tell anyone interested in this business that the *best* textbook of public relations still costs just 25¢ daily and $1.00 on Sunday." He picks up a copy of the New York *Times* to punctuate his point.

Public relations requires lots of enthusiasm and initiative. You can't be afraid to telephone people you have never met or whose names are followed by impressive titles like "Managing Editor" and "News Director," and you can't be reluctant to call —again and again—a person who never seems to have time to talk to you. Public relations requires, above all, persistence, persuasiveness, and diplomacy. There is a particularly apt Yiddish word that describes another quality a P.R. person needs in his or her profile of useful traits; that word is *chutzpa* (pronounced HOUTZ-puh), which was defined by Leo Rosten in *The Joys of Yiddish* as "Gall, brazen nerve, effrontery, incredible 'guts.'" To which can be added this comment by a young P.R. executive, "In terms of personality, you must walk the line between being forceful, but not aggressive. You have to sell yourself and be charming, yet the line between forcefulness and aggression—or passivity—is often very fine."

WHERE ARE THE JOBS IN PUBLIC RELATIONS?

PRSA reports that as we enter the eighties, people in public relations work number an estimated 70,000 or more, reflecting a growth rate over the past quarter century that might be higher

than that of any other management function. Why so rapid and
large a growth? The increasing dependence on good communications in order to survive and grow in this fast-moving
complex world, has resulted, more and more, in the person responsible for public relations being a corporate officer. In turn,
this has created a P.R. function in almost every field and
profession—in business, industry, government, education, nonprofit organizations, sports and entertainment and even the mil-
itary. The needs are obvious, the jobs are there and the career
potential is almost unlimited, but how do *you* get started?

When asked about entry-level job opportunities in public
relations, Richard Weiner, President of Richard Weiner, Inc.,
first clarified that the field encompasses all of the public information specialists' jobs in Washington and that, in fact, Uncle
Sam is the *largest* employer of P.R. people in the United States.
"Second largest is the nonprofit sector—the AMA (American
Medical Association), National Farm Bureau, colleges,
churches, and that type of thing. Third are corporations; and
they really offer the best possibility for good entry-level jobs.

"You'll find many young people at the entry level in corporate P.R. jobs these days; some of them are writing corporate
newsletters, preparing annual reports, working for special projects—it's all P.R." (In fact, in corporations, P.R. activity goes
under a variety of names that indicate the function: public information, corporate communicator, public or community
affairs, employee relations, internal communications, investor
relations, marketing or product publicity, etc.)

ADVICE FOR GETTING INTO PUBLIC RELATIONS

Linda Taber, who heads Carol Moberg Communications, a
subsidiary of Ketchum MacLeod & Grove Public Relations,
specializing in food and consumer product public relations,
stresses that the ability to write well is essential. "Once you
have a job, learn everything you can and practice your writing,
and, most important, *read*. To be successful you have to know
your media; you have to know what's happening that you can
tie-in to; you have to watch what's being done and relate it to

what you can do for a client." Linda suggests searching for an entry-level job with the large agencies because they have the time to train beginners, but she points out that most places either have a "promote or not to promote from within policy" which is easy to check out. You *know* the best kind of place to go with.

"I also think small newspapers, weeklies or dailies, are good places to start," Linda Taber continues. "When the profession first gained importance, most P.R. people were ex-newspaper men or women. There was good reason. P.R. is communicating on every level, externally and internally, and few places offer you more opportunity to write every day and hone your skills than does a newspaper."

Lory Roston, who heads his own firm specializing in public relations, as well as personal public relations for corporate executives, agrees with Linda. "Public Relations is communicating, and communicating means writing—proposals, letters, reports, story suggestions, sometimes the stories themselves to appear under your client's name, speeches, annual reports and whatever it takes to get the job done.

"If you want to succeed in this field, start wherever you have to, doing whatever you have to and take the job for 'zilch' if you have to. Then do more than what is asked of you and learn while doing it." A course in practical business writing is useful according to Lory, and he also suggests getting a head start on job-hunting.

"Try writing to the heads of major P.R. firms while you're still in school. Tell them you're interested in working for them when you graduate, so you want to know what courses you should take and what skills you need to acquire from them. If you achieve something outstanding in college, keep them advised. It all helps when you finally go knocking on their company door for a job."

Charlotte Kelly, Vice-President/Corporate Communications, Charter Publishing Company (*Ladies' Home Journal, Redbook,* and *Sport* magazines) says, "P.R. practitioners get paid for four things—time, work, experience, and contacts." Since a newcomer to the field usually doesn't have the experience or contacts, he or she can only offer the willingness to put in lots of time and hard work to gain the experience and make the contacts. Charlotte, who started in the business as a secretary, as did her boss at the time, Helen Gurley Brown (now Editor of *Cosmopolitan* magazine), still thinks beginners need a few special skills—good typing and reasonable shorthand—that will answer their employer's immediate needs.

Then she advises, "Do everything you *have* to do to get a job in a professional P.R. environment and when you do get it, do everything you *can* do on that job to learn and everything you should do on that job to get promoted. There's nothing new about that formula: fill a need, do what you can do beyond the needs and do what you should do to be noticed and promoted. One difference today is that you can be up front about your ambition. Once earned, you can ask for that promotion instead of waiting for it to be bestowed upon you . . . and it doesn't take as long as it used to."

RoseMarie Brooks, Public Relations and Promotion Director of *Sport* magazine, views public relations as one of the important tools of communications and marketing. "Like everyone else, I think writing is one of the most important skills for a career in public relations, but I also think judgment is an indispensable qualification. The ability to define a problem, and find a practical solution, is what real public relations is all about. And, people going into public relations and promotion should be aware of the unending, nitty gritty detail it takes to produce a simple press conference, a new product introduction, or a special event. Behind all the glamour, there's a lot of hard work and a great need for organization. Seeing the broad picture isn't enough. To really be successful, you've got to have the ability to put together all the pieces painstakingly, one at a time . . . and be prepared to have everyone think the job was easy when it's over. Because that's how it should appear—smooth and without effort."

Does it all sound pretty much the same? It is. And what it adds up to is hard work, a willingness to extend yourself to learn a job that is multifaceted.

But when you interview for either an assistant or secretarial position, you have to be more specific about your abilities and interests. Just saying that you want to learn public relations isn't enough if you have no concept of what public relations involves.

FUNCTIONS IN PUBLIC RELATIONS

There are a lot of different functions in this business and most jobs involve one or more of these functions, so it should be easy to find one that fits your interests and skills. The following specific functions, as defined by the Public Relations Society of America, can give you some guidance in asking for a job you want:

PROGRAMMING

This involves analyzing problems and opportunities, defining goals and the publics (or groups of people whose support or understanding is needed), and recommending and planning activities. It may require budgeting and assignment of responsibilities to the appropriate people, including nonpublic relations personnel. For example, an organization's president or executive director is often a key figure in public relations activities.

RELATIONSHIPS

Successful public relations people develop skill in personally gathering information from management, from colleagues in their organizations, and from external sources. Continually evaluating what they have learned, they formulate recommendations and gain approval for them from their managements.

Many public relations activities require working with, and sometimes through, other functions, including personnel, legal, and marketing staffs. The practitioner who learns to be persuasive with others will be most effective.

Public relations people also represent their organizations. Sometimes this is formal, in which they are an official representative to a trade or professional association. But in all their relationships with others—including people in industry groups, regulatory agencies and government, educational institutions, and the general public—public relations personnel are "at work" in behalf of their organizations.

WRITING AND EDITING

Since the public relations worker is often trying to reach large groups of people, the tool most often used is the printed word. Examples of its use are found in reports, news releases, booklets, speeches, film scripts, trade magazine articles, product information and technical material, employee publications, newsletters, shareholder reports and other management communications, directed to both organization personnel and external groups. A sound, clear style of writing, which effectively communicates, is virtually a must for public relations work.

INFORMATION

Setting up channels for the dissemination of material to appropriate newspaper, broadcast, general and trade publication editors, and contact with them in such a way as to enlist their interest in using an organization's news and features, are normal public relations activities. This requires a knowledge of how newspapers and other media operate, the areas of specialization of publications and the interests of individual editors. Competition is keen for the attention of editors and broadcasters who have a limited amount of space and time at their disposal. As one public relations practitioner puts it, "You have to get to the right story at the right time." Although ideas are accepted on the basis of news worthiness and other readership value, an ability to develop relationships of mutual respect and cooperation with the press can be useful to both the practitioner and the newsman.

PRODUCTION

Brochures, special reports, films, and multimedia programs

are important ways of communicating. The public relations practitioner need not be an expert in art, layout, typography, and photography, but background knowledge of the techniques of preparation is needed for intelligent planning and supervision of their use.

SPECIAL EVENTS

News conferences, convention exhibits and special showings, new facility and anniversary celebrations, contest and award programs, tours, and special meetings make only a partial list of the special events used to gain the attention and acceptance of groups of people. They involve careful planning and coordination, attention to detail, preparation of special booklets, publicity and reports.

SPEAKING

Public relations work often requires skill in face-to-face communication—finding appropriate platforms, the preparation of speeches for others, and the delivery of speeches. The person who can effectively address individuals and groups will enjoy the advantage over those whose facility of expression is limited to writing.

RESEARCH AND EVALUATION

The first activity undertaken by a public relations practitioner is always fact-gathering. As previously indicated, this can be highly personal, through interviews, review of library materials and informal conversations. It can also involve the use of survey techniques and firms specializing in designing and conducting opinion research.

After a program is completed, the public relations practitioner should study its results and make an evaluation about the program's implementation and effectiveness. Managements are increasingly expecting such research and evaluation from their public relations advisers.

WHERE CAN YOU GO IN PUBLIC RELATIONS?

In most businesses (including the other media professions), complex organization diagrams indicate how one job title follows another and how departments within a corporation relate to each other. In public relations, the diagraming is a bit more difficult because the departments are set up to meet the needs of the individual agency or corporation. Generally, P.R. people, no matter how high up, are one-man bands. They are people who enjoy filling a variety of roles single-handedly that in an advertising agency, would usually be divided among several specialists. Whether you are the P.R. Director of a major corporation or a V.P. and Account Executive in a P.R. agency, you will do much of your own media and market research, write your own copy, prepare your own proposals, maintain your own contacts and do your own follow-up. As a result, the P.R. department of a large company may consist of only one or two executives and a secretary, or the director or communicator could have several departments—advertising, public relations, employee relations—all under his or her direction. Large P.R. agencies operate with a seemingly minimal number of departments and subdepartments, and fewer support services than advertising agencies.

Your progress in a P.R. career, then, might be less a matter of moving through a long series of job titles and more a matter of progress measured by the type and number of projects handled and the scope of your responsibilities (such as supervising). On the corporate side, particularly, the best and perhaps only likely entry-level opportunity is secretarial or clerical (even if the title is Assistant to the Public Relations Director). Bob DeLay, President of the Direct Mail/Marketing Association, says, however, "You can make a lot more out of any job you take. If I were hired as an assistant, I would do more than I was asked to do. I would look for opportunities where I could show initiative and imagination. I would be willing to work beyond what my responsibilities were. And I wouldn't be afraid to tell people that I was doing this as a stepping stone, that I want to get ahead. After all, who could turn away a worker who is assertive and responsible and looks for additional work?"

And one ex-secretary, who is now a P.R. Director, had this to say, "Serving in those entry-level positions, you have an opportunity to learn how new product introductions are developed, the timing of your work—for example, that new-product stories have to be planned three to four months ahead of their release. This is the key in this field—learning how to apportion your time, to do the advance work which is so important, and then to adhere to your schedule, while doing current follow-up on a daily basis with local newspaper people. On the corporate level, the best starting spot is an administrative assistant or secretarial spot, working your way up."

The secretarial or assistant's level is an equally good starting point in a P.R. agency, as well. In such cases, you may work on one account or on five or six different accounts (depending upon the size of the agency and the scope of the accounts) and you may work for one or several account executives. An agency spot, however, is the best place to get an overview of different approaches used for different types of clients; it adds more grist to the mill, so to speak, when you get up to the level where you have your own accounts to handle and need to do what Richard Weiner talked about, putting ideas together from various sources.

Once you do get to be an account executive in a P.R. agency, you may at first have only one large or perhaps two smaller accounts. As you gain more experience, you will be assigned more projects and more clients until you eventually are supervising and maybe adding a vice-presidency after your name. Then, before you know it, you could have your own agency.

A medium-size public relations agency

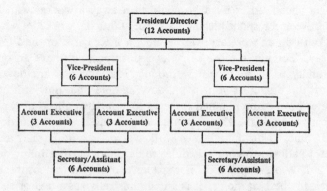

A large public relations agency

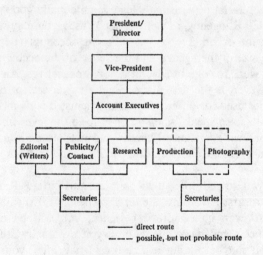

A corporate public relations department

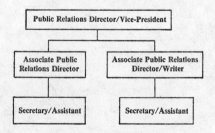

BREAKING INTO PUBLIC RELATIONS: A VIEW FROM THE INSIDE

A 26-year-old account executive with a New York public relations agency, who had been headed for a career as an advertising copywriter—or so she thought—until she took a night course in P.R. at The New School for Social Research on the suggestion of a boss who thought she would be suited to the field. Then, as she excitedly puts it, "I found P.R., and P.R. found me."

Public Relations found her when she was shopping one Saturday for additions to her collection of antique boxes. "I got to talking with the woman who owned the shop and she told me about a fashion show she was having for Valentine's Day—she has lovely antique clothing, too—and that she wanted a lot of people to come. Diane Keaton has bought from her, and people like that, because she rents clothes for films, but she said she really needed to get her name around more. Well, I was taking my P.R. course at The New School then, so I said, half kidding, 'What you need is a P.R. person. Like me.' Well, her eyes lit up and she said, 'Would you? Are you in P.R.?' At that point, my heart went 'clunk,' but just like I had learned in class, in the P.R. business you have to stay cool and handle everything with a lot of assurance, so I didn't say 'no' about being in P.R., I just said—and looking back I can't believe I did it—I just said, *very* professionally, 'Why don't you let me put together a proposal for you?' "

She spent the next three nights after work writing a proposal and used the weekend to put together a notebook of all the local New York media (magazines big and small; neighborhood newspapers and the major dailies; all the radio and television stations); she also drafted a release to show her new "client." "The hardest part," she confides, "was figuring out what to charge. But I asked everyone I knew for advice and I called my P.R. teacher. I probably ended up making about 25¢ an hour on that job, I spent so much time on it—but you do that when you start out, I guess. And it paid off! I even got her the Style page of the New York *Times!* It took me three months and a lot of phone calls, but I got it!"

This success with her "antique lady," as she calls her first client, started a snowball rolling. The antique lady had a cousin in the fashion business who needed publicity to help sell to the big department stores, and the cousin knew a new restaurant that wanted to do something unique for its opening. Meanwhile, there was an art show sponsored by a big client of the ad agency she worked for (she was secretary to the creative director) and a friend there had a friend who wanted to publicize her appearance as a flamenco dancer.

But it wasn't all roses. One client was ten minutes late for an interview, TV coverage never materialized for the restaurant opening, and a few bills were difficult to collect, but within six months there was a scrapbook full of "clips" (published news items mentioning her clients) and, as she puts it, "enough money for a really terrific trip to Paris!"

She never got to Paris in the fall as she planned, however. In May she had her first interview in the P.R. field and, although she didn't get that job, the experience convinced her of one thing: "You survived the interview, you're ready." In June, she interviewed for her current job after contacting one of the guest speakers from her class. "It was a chance, but in P.R. you try everything." By October, just eleven months after first meeting her "antique lady," she was in South America as the sole escort for a press trip she had organized. "It's hard work being an account executive in P.R. You do everything! With that trip, for instance, I had to negotiate with the airline, I chose the journalists we would invite, handled their hotels and things. But I have a terrific boss, who's been in the business a long time. And we talk a lot. He's really helpful, and around him I can be excited or I can be depressed. But, like he says, 'So, you didn't get the Chicago *Tribune;* call the *Daily News.*'"

To anyone looking for a way into the field, she says, "Meet anyone—everyone. So that even if you're too inexperienced now, you won't be in two years. Above all, remember people—contacts. And it's called knowing-what-you-want." The phone on her desk rings, but before answering, she adds, "I'm working on a proposal for a wine account; this is a list of editors I have to call about last week's press conference; I'm still collecting clips from that trip to South America. Plus, now," she whispers, "they've hinted about putting me on *another* account! I don't know how much more I can handle, but I love it!"

On the other hand, a corporate public relations executive relates, "I was a secretary when I created my own entry-level position that led me to my present job as Director of Publicity, National and International (for a major perfumer). I really came in through the back door. I didn't know what I wanted to do. I began as an administrative assistant to the president of the firm. I had an English Lit background, with some publicity and journalism, and I knew I wanted to incorporate writing into my career, whether as a copywriter or in public relations." She pauses, "I'm sure people today have a much better idea of planning goals and what a future career is all about, but I'm just now beginning to understand what that means. When I came to New York, I investigated magazines and then really just came upon this field. When I got here, I was promised by my boss that I would be promoted within a certain number of years. At first, I waited for him to make the appropriate moves. Then, after a while, I realized that *he* wanted *me* to tell *him* what I wanted to do, and until I was ready to do that, it wouldn't happen.

"So I proceeded to make my own show. I decided to become involved in the P.R. area, although I viewed it at the time as somewhat of a turn-off. I saw it as luncheons, people trying to be powerful. And fluff! It also seemed as if the P.R. department was fully staffed. So I created my own job. I wrote an outline for a job I called Public Affairs/Public Information, which many companies have, but didn't exist here. I presented my idea and the president of the company in turn presented it to the woman who is now my boss. They were both impressed, and took my proposal before a P.R. Department meeting. However, they did not offer me *that* job, but made me Manager of the perfume for the U.S.A. Division—which was *better* than I asked for. After a year and a half in that position, I was made Director of U.S.A. *and* International—where I am now."

DOING YOUR HOMEWORK IN PUBLIC RELATIONS

Since P.R. is a field where one has to communicate, there is no better way to learn about it than from people who write about their experiences in it. Here are just a few of the books you'll enjoy and learn from.

ADVANCE READING

Walking the Tightrope: The Private Confessions of a Public Relations Man by Henry C. Rogers (William Morrow, New York, 1980): Stories and anecdotes by a forty-year veteran of the business; "a light, lay version of what the public relations business is really like."

Critical Issues in Public Relations by Hill & Knowlton executives (Prentice-Hall, Englewood Cliffs, 1975): May be advanced for you at this stage, but the foreword includes an introduction to P.R., the historic roots of the business, and the essence of communications; also, each section of the book is written by an executive of Hill & Knowlton (largest P.R. agency in the world), who is an expert in his or her field.

AFTER YOU GET THE JOB

Professional's Guide to Publicity by Richard Weiner (Richard Weiner, Inc., New York, 1978): The introduction offers this book as a "work manual" for a "working publicist" with a "working press"; chapters cover many of "how-to's" for specific situations (time pegs, press kits, release formats, mailings, etc.). Overall, a concise, direct, clean presentation of the steps of good P.R.

The Right Angles (How to Do Successful Publicity) by Babette Hall (Ives Washburn, Inc., div. of David McKay, New York, 1965): A thorough book on the mechanics, strategies, and techniques of public relations. Although not recent, it gives a sound idea of the operations.

Effective Public Relations by Scott M. Cutlip & Allen H. Center, Fifth Ed. (Prentice-Hall, Englewood Cliffs, 1978)

Your Future in Public Relations by Edward L. Bernays
(Richards Rosen Press, New York, 1964)

Your Career in P.R. by Jody Donahue (Julian Messner,
New York, 1967)

The Nature of Public Relations by John E. Marston
(McGraw-Hill, New York, 1963)

KEY TRADE PUBLICATIONS

Public Relations Journal ($20 per year; 845 Third Avenue, New York, NY 10022)

The Publicist ($15 per year; P.R. Aids, Inc., 221 Park
Avenue South, New York, NY 10003): Bimonthly, includes interviews with professionals and a section called
"Craft," with up-dates on the "nuts and bolts" of doing
P.R.

Public Relations News ($127.50 a year; 127 East 80th
Street, New York, NY 10021): Costly, but widely read in
the field.

CAREER INFORMATION

Public Relations Society of America, Inc., PRSA Career
Guidance, 845 Third Avenue, New York, NY 10022.

U. S. Dept. of Labor, Wage and Labor Standards Administration, Washington, D.C.

Chapter 10

RADIO AND TELEVISION BROADCASTING, FILM FOR TELEVISION, CABLE TELEVISION AND HOME VIDEO

WHAT IS IT ALL ABOUT?

Broadcasting, like publishing, is in the business of communicating news, ideas, and entertainment. But in this case, the forms are audio or audio-visual and the means is electronic. There's no paper, no ink, nothing tangible. As one newscaster is reputed to have remarked with a tone of regret, "No one ever rereads the six o'clock news."

Yet broadcasting is an omnipresent communication medium and the largest (and if you say disdainfully that you never watch television or listen to the radio, you have no business even reading this chapter). It is classical music on the clock radio in the morning and Johnny Carson's jokes before bed at night; it's live video coverage of world events as they happen and stereo simulcasts—on both radio and television—of great opera live from the Metropolitan Opera; it's the World Series, the Super Bowl and decades of "I Love Lucy" reruns; it's laugh-a-minute situation comedies and sob-a-minute soap operas; it's game shows, talk shows, and religion by satellite; it's shrieking DJs on Top-40 rock stations and mellow-voiced late-night poetry readers on FM; and it is feature films being shown in your living room. The broadcasting industry is our source of nonstop, instant information and entertainment, and its products are readily available at the touch of a switch.

Broadcasting people love the magic of their business and have few regrets that their audience has nothing tangible to place on a shelf and gather dust (*although the arrival of video discs and video recordings is about to change all that*). They know that the business they are in is show business and that the *performance* is the key to communication, and not necessarily the written material that leads up to it. They also know, and relish, the fact that they can reach more people at one time, in one minute, than other media forms can reach in a week (newspapers), or a month (magazines), or a year (books). It is estimated that on any given winter week night at 9 P.M., as many as 115 million Americans are watching television; add to that number the millions more who are listening to the radio—in a car or on a skateboard, while washing the dinner dishes or studying for the next day's algebra test—and it becomes easy to understand how the term "mass media" evolved and became synonymous with the broadcasting industry.

RADIO AND ITS COMPETITOR, TELEVISION

Although radio broadcasting was utilized during the years of World War I, it wasn't until 1919 that the ban on private broadcasting was lifted. Even then, it was nearly a decade before radio executives saw the mass-marketing possibilities of this medium. And then, radio reigned supreme for about a quarter of a century. In the late 1940s, commercial television made its appearance (although it's been around on an experimental basis since the 1920s), and many people felt that radio was doomed. And, for a while, it did indeed appear that unless radio broadcasters changed their content and technique, the industry might have actually faded away.

Fortunately for radio, the Federal Communications Commission put a freeze on station licensing until the early 1950s (while the FCC worked out a nationwide plan for telecasting), and to a large extent, this gave radio executives the needed time to redevelop this medium. So radio, as a matter of survival, underwent a revolution. First of all, its programming was radically changed. Secondly, the transistor enabled manufacturers to completely transform radios from big, bulky equipment to the miniportables that we know today. These two factors did more to ensure the growth and development of radio as a mass medium than anything else. Today, there are nearly 8000 radio stations which broadcast daily in America, and approximately 400 million radio sets. In addition, a "recent action by the Federal Communications Commission mandated 140 new low-power community television stations to be 'dropped in' between existing stations. Other legislation opened the radio bands for 125 more stations," according to the New York *Times* survey "Occupational Outlooks."

The challenge of the broadcasting business, then, is twofold. First, because most radio and television stations in this country now operate on eighteen- to twenty-four-hour-per-day schedules, three hundred sixty-five days a year, there is the challenge of filling all of those hours with good programming. Second, there is the challenge of communicating with many different people at one time, of producing something that can be understood, appreciated, and accepted both by a farmer in Iowa and a professor in Boston, or, as is particularly true in the case of local radio, by residents of luxury neighborhoods as well as by those in the ghettos.

In the old days of radio (and now in television) that double challenge produced what is known in the business as "middle of the road" programming and resulted in a "mixed-bag" approach to filling the hours of air time. (Ask your parents what it was like to *listen* to a situation comedy or a soap opera.) But as the introduction of television forced the radio side of broadcasting to develop new forms of programming, radio had to alter its "middle of the road," general formats and tailor its programming to the needs, tastes, and interests of *specifically defined* groups of listeners (i.e., Country-Western, Jazz, Disco, Foreign Language, or Progressive).

Some industry-watchers of broadcasting now predict that the emerging industries of video storage (video recorders and video discs) and cable/Pay-TV will have a similar effect on commercial television broadcasting—specialization, or what some call "narrowcasting." Perhaps this will be true; perhaps not. But as a former public access (*cable*) talk-show hostess once remarked when asked where television is going, "Oh, God! It's a moving target; open for anyone!"

WHO GETS THE JOBS IN BROADCASTING?

Leaving cable aside for the moment, traditional commercial broadcasting is one of the toughest businesses there is to break into, particularly if you have your sights set on one of the "glamour" jobs like announcer, producer, reporter, writer, or director. Benita Fury, Consumer Affairs Reporter for WNBC-TV in New York, quips, "There are only fifty of us in the entire business and we just keep trading jobs."

"The biggest problem with young people today," says Robert M. Silverman, head of a New York based broadcast barter advertising agency, "is that they all want to be announcers, DJs, and on-the-air personalities. They may have had some experience on their college radio station, or they may have even put together a demo tape. But generally, these youngsters are setting themselves up for disappointment, because most likely, whatever they've done doesn't amount to a hill of beans."

Robert Silverman, who is also chairman of a New York metropolitan radio station, continues, "Now, that's not to say they can't get into radio, they should just understand the facts of life. Kids wanting to be radio personalities are a dime a dozen. That's a fact. It's also a fact that if you can get almost *any* kind of job in radio, and you're willing to work hard, then you can turn it into an opportunity. Tell your employer that you'll do anything, but that you'd also like an opportunity to work on the air. Volunteer for a graveyard slot—one that no one else wants. Or else tell them you'll be on call twenty-four hours a day in case anyone gets sick.

"Hang around the station and learn everything there is to know. Make demonstration tapes, help with recording commercials, logging them and such. Before you know it, you'll know a lot about radio and you'll actually be able to make a contribution."

Thomas Moore, former President of ABC-TV network and now head of his own film production company, explains why he thinks there are so many young people interested in careers in broadcasting.

"I think electronic media holds a special fascination for young people. They've grown up completely surrounded by television, movies, radio—when you think about it, people under the age of thirty have never known a life without TV. They're very attracted to the media, very excited by it and they want to have a hand in it. As a result it's very competitive. For every job available, there might be at least a dozen people to whom you'd want to give the job, because they're all that good and that qualified. Then, when you consider that there are very few entry-level positions available that require 'zero' experience and very few training programs . . ." he shakes his head, "you begin to get an idea of what goes on in broadcasting.

"Broadcasting is a highly profit-oriented operation," continues Thomas Moore. "In my position people will sometimes ask me to talk to a son or daughter about the field, and usually their attitude, when they come in, is, 'How do I get into the business?' But when they approach it like that, I'm inclined to be very negative with them. And I don't paint a positive picture because they're missing the point. Unless they make a relationship to profitability and performance, what interest should I take in them? That's one of the few things young people know how to do—to let people know they're interested in making profits."

He then offers this advice: "Any time you pitch a job, approach it positively and sell your assets. You can tell them what you did in college or high school and how you made profits at it. Even if your experience is 'zero,' you can still position yourself positively. For example, you can sell yourself as a TV watcher—that you've been watching it every day since you were eight years old. Or, if you're someone who has watched thousands of hours of sports, you can go into an interview and tell your prospective employer that. And then you can go on and say that you've got plenty of ideas that could make a lot of money for sports on TV. That's what's going to sell you. Showing that you're thinking and that you're thinking about profits and how to make them, that's how you're going to get a job. They're interested in people with ideas, drive, understanding. And they want self-starters.

"If you're entering one of these fields, you've got to make up your mind that it's not going to be easy. It takes time. That's the way it is. And don't be frightened by rejection. Look at every interview as a chance to better you and your technique, rather than as a rejection. Then, just keep working on contacts. Every time you talk with someone, find out if there's someone you can speak to and if you can use their name. Sooner or later, something will give. But, remember, when you go into any interview for an entry-level position, or any position, make it clear that you know what you want, even if you're not really sure. You can't just go in and say, 'Well, I want to work in film for a year or two to see what I want to do.' No one wants to pay you to case the joint."

WHAT ARE THE JOBS IN RADIO AND TELEVISION?

Unlike some of the other mass communications fields, broadcasting often offers the best entry-level positions *out of town*. Getting a start at a small radio station can provide you with opportunities to really learn how a station works—experience that can pay off later when you show a potential employer that you understand and can contribute to company profits.

At a small-town radio station, it is not at all unusual to combine a number of different job title responsibilities into one position. As a result, you might keep the station log, sell commercial time to prospective advertisers, write copy, and even make announcements! It is almost impossible for an individual to get this kind of experience at a large station in a big city.

"Many people don't realize it," says Robert Silverman, "but there is a crying need in radio for sales people. I don't know of a station any place that doesn't need sales people. However, there is no reason in the world for a station to take a complete neophyte and guarantee him a good salary and expenses. So, if you want a job, you've got to sweeten the deal. Go to any small-town station and offer to work on straight commission. There are very few stations in small markets that would turn down a sales person with proper qualifications. And by that I mean well-spoken, well-dressed and with no chip on your shoulder."

Broadcasting (like theatrical film) is one of the most difficult fields to break into, because it does not have the number of entry-level positions that are required in the other media fields. That's why it is so important to take *any* job you are offered. Unlike many of the other communications professions where some jobs just don't track, broadcasting is still so young that the industry is not highly structured. About the only kinds of jobs that could offer problems in movement would be the lateral (or even downward) moves *out* of a union job. If you're required to join a union in order to get the job, check it out carefully for career tracking.

Large station or small, big city or rural community, how do you create opportunities? "My advice is simply this," Thomas Moore continues, "do anything to get your nose in that tent, whether it's packing and shipping film or working in the mailroom. It doesn't matter—just do anything to get in." He then explained how it works, "Many places hire from within and anytime a job opens up it will be posted all over the house—not just in the corporate offices, but in the warehouses and the studios. So, even if you have a job at the bottom of the barrel, all you have to do is keep your eyes peeled and you will find these posted. They don't look outside unless there are absolutely no takers on the inside.

"When you take *any* job in media, it means that you're there to take advantage of the next best offer. People know that when you go in as a shipping clerk in the film industry, you're not there to make a career of being a shipping clerk. You're there to gain experience that will let you sell yourself a little higher up the next time. The minute you get on the scene, look for what has to be done, above and beyond the call of duty. Do it and make sure someone is around to see you doing it. Make sure someone sees you and tells other people about you. And the higher up you go in trying to show people what you can do, the better. Expect that wherever you enter you'll be at a very, very low level. But to compensate, once you get there, set your sights high and get to know people. Contacts are the name of the game."

"Get out of town for about five years," is the advice of a successful veteran on-camera reporter, "or get yourself a specialty and try to make a name for yourself in that specialty in the "boonies," in a newspaper or by writing a book. It also doesn't hurt if you *look* like someone who is already on the air. Everybody is either a Walter Cronkite-type or a Barbara Walters-type or looks like the anchor person on the competing station—and *every* sports announcer in the country sounds like Howard Cosell."

WHERE CAN YOU GO IN RADIO AND TELEVISION?

Whether you work for a local station, or one of the big national networks, the corporate set-up in broadcasting is essentially the same, and somewhat like a giant pinwheel. Management is the center, the pin, and the individual blades that whirl around it are the four key departments of engineering, sales, news, and programming.

Within each of these areas there are, of course, possibilities for moving up the ladder, say from Program Manager to Program Director to Station Manager, but the broadcasting and its supporting film businesses are essentially built on individual specialties. Announcers are announcers, camerapeople are camerapeople, and only occasionally do music librarians venture away from their record collections toward the executive suite. *Career tracking in broadcasting and film is more a matter of tenure and seniority than it is of moving through a formalized system of job titles or vice-presidencies and movement tends to be from station to station, network to network or city to city, as opposed to internally.*

TECHNICAL

Before you begin to dream of a career in broadcasting, there are a few other things you should know about career tracking in these businesses. On the technical side, for instance, it's vital that you realize that—unless you are trained and have already worked out a union apprenticeship for yourself—you can practically forget about going into engineering or any of the technical specialists' jobs in commercial broadcasting or film, such as film/tape editor, cameraperson, audio engineer, make-up, etc. That side of the businesses is one of those *"you've-got-to-have-your-union-card-to-work-and-you've-got-to-work-to-get-your-union-card"* situations, and union membership openings tend to be passed along on a legacy basis.

Getting Practical Experience for Television and Film: Non-Theatrical Film   For more than fifty years, non-theatrical (non-entertainment) films have existed as a means of reaching a specific audience to communicate information and ideas. The majority of these films have been underwritten by business, but special interest groups (such as the government, education, health, religious and medical) are all finding new and innovative uses for non-theatrical films and continue to be big users.

Non-theatrical filmmaking accounts for its popularity because it can deliver specific messages to specific groups. "We have produced films for a group as small as fifty," according to Jay Rubin, producer for Caribiner, Inc., an East Coast production house, "because more and more businesses and special interest groups are finding that audio-visual productions can be a great way to motivate people." It fulfills such tasks as fundraising, product demonstrations, dissemination of information to minority groups, third world countries and much more. Industry, the biggest users, utilize non-theatrical film as a means to promote corporate public relations (outreach films), to stimulate a sales force, to introduce new corporate sales programs, etc.

In the past, most non-theatrical films have been produced on filmstrips and slides, often with an accompanying script. Today, sync slide tape productions and filmstrips are the most common form of non-theatrical film, although 16mm and 35mm moving film are used for more elaborate (and costly) film productions.

The last ten years have seen a tremendous change in this industry as it relates to corporate use. Companies are no longer underwriting simple filmstrips for employee use, but instead, they are looking to much more elaborate productions known in the trade as "shows." Producing non-theatrical audio-visual shows can cost anywhere from $10,000–$1.5 million and more. The average major production costs about $100,000 and you can double that cost if live talent is to be used.

"Multi-image productions and the use of live talent are now the rage," Jay Rubin continues. "Management is starting to realize that intracompany communications can have real financial rewards. It used to be that company meetings were considered adequate if a flip chart and a recording were used in the company conference room. Now, company meetings are planned in off-site locations and they are 'staged' to meet very specific corporate objectives. For example, a company may want to motivate their sales force, or introduce a new product, or educate their employees concerning consumer relations or even to encourage optimism after a particularly bad year."

The non-theatrical film business is no longer limited to just stills and moving film. It is a mushrooming field that many times resembles a Broadway theater production more closely than it does an ordinary filmstrip. "Businesses want entertainment with a slant towards a corporate objective," says Jay Rubin. "And that is precisely why they are now using multi-image projections with as many as twenty-one screens and live talent in these productions."

Recently, Caribiner produced a traveling show for one of the top *Fortune* 500 companies. The purpose of this presentation was to establish a better rapport with their dealers around the country. This particular show, which cost more than $1 million to produce, made seven appearances and was billed as a three-act comedy. As part of the presentation, there were several three-screen multi-image pieces, which included a video puppet of the company mascot which acted as an MC! Members of management gave speeches and Caribiner provided the slides and film needed to support these discussions. In addition, Caribiner designed and created all the necessary staging and sets.

Each year, approximately 15,000 non-theatrical films are produced in the United States by an estimated 1200 firms spread

from coast to coast. Although most of the firms that produce
these films are relatively small (in comparison with those which
produce entertainment films), *they provide an opportunity for
both creative expression and fairly rapid career tracking once
you break in.* Unlike the broadcasting industry where it is often
necessary to track from a small station in a small town to a medium station in a medium town and on upwards, the non-theatrical film industry is still so young that it allows for an incredible learning opportunity within the company.

"It is very helpful to have a background in either film, theater or video," Jay continues, "but if you haven't had that
specific training, then I suggest you take some specialized
courses. Study photo-journalism and get a camera. In many
ways there is a lot of similarity between photo-journalism and
filmmaking because they both tell a story with pictures. If you
like to write, then find a project and write something. Or else be
prepared to show a prospective employer tapes or credits and
samples of films on which you've worked."

Jay Rubin wasn't always a producer. Jay, who is still in his
twenties, had his basic training in arts. "My first job was as a
graphic designer. Part of my responsibility was to design slides
for production houses. I found it so interesting that I decided
I'd like to do audio-visual, film, and video production work on
a full-time basis. I went to work for Caribiner, learned the
ropes and now I'm a full producer. This is a young business
with a lot of young people, and if you're willing to work hard
and can contribute, well, you can practically write your own
ticket."

"This field is wide open with opportunities," says another
young producer in non-theatrical films. "But the working style is
quite a bit different in this industry than in many others. It's important to be a generalist. You've got to know how to sell, how
to be creative, and how to produce for your studio's bottom
line.

"To be a good writer or a good designer simply isn't enough.
Most of those people are hired on a freelance basis anyway.
These studios are small, and that in itself requires you to wear
many different hats.

"I never dreamed that this kind of filmmaking could be so creative. My professors never told me that I could be choreographing live talent for a major oil company. But that's exactly what I did last week. I guess you could say that industrial films have come a long way."

PROGRAMMING AND PRODUCTION

Unions complicate the issues of entry and advancement on the programming and production sides of broadcasting and film as well, but less so than that of technical. The jobs, for example, of newscaster, staff announcer, director, writer, and producer are unionized at most stations and film production houses, and *always* are at the major ones. Getting the work experience to qualify for the union card in these areas is less difficult too, there are fewer instances of controlled apprenticeships to overcome.

One of the few non-unionized areas of broadcasting is Sales, and Thomas Moore maintains, "knowing how to sell will maximize your creative talents in terms of understanding profitability." On the other hand, however, sales is a specialty (and a potentially lucrative one since it is a salary-plus-commission job), but if you have your heart set on programming/production —the creative side of the broadcasting or film business—there is no clear and easy path to follow out of sales, particularly beyond the early stages. You simply must continue to keep yourself aware of what's being posted in the house.

Broadcasting may sound like a pretty tough field to break into, and it is, but don't be discouraged! There is so much change going on in the industry today, that broadcasting is spawning branch businesses where opportunities are practically boundless!

Radio/TV Station

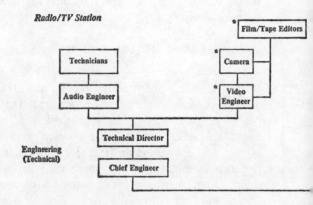

* Film/Tape Editors

Technicians

* Camera

Audio Engineer

* Video Engineer

Engineering
(Technical)

Technical Director

Chief Engineer

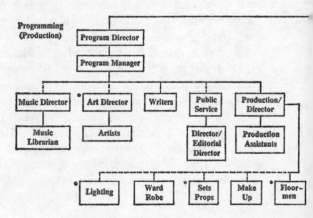

Programming
(Production)

Program Director

Program Manager

Music Director

* Art Director

Writers

Public Service

Production/Director

Music Librarian

Artists

Director/Editorial Director

Production Assistants

* Lighting

Ward Robe

* Sets Props

Make Up

* Floor-men

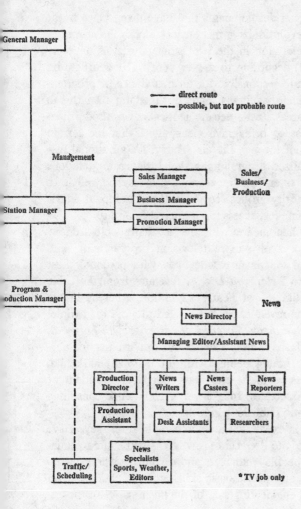

General Manager

direct route
possible, but not probable route

Management

Station Manager

Sales Manager

Business Manager

Promotion Manager

Sales/
Business/
Production

Program &
Production Manager

News

News Director

Managing Editor/Assistant News

Production
Director

News
Writers

News
Casters

News
Reporters

Production
Assistant

Desk Assistants

Researchers

Traffic/
Scheduling

News
Specialists
Sports, Weather,
Editors

* TV job only

BROADCAST TELEVISION'S COMPETITOR, CABLE

The technological developments that have taken place in the last decade are revolutionizing this business. With the advent of the satellite, acceleration in the television industry is unprecedented. Satellites, according to a New York *Times* article on cable television, are responsible for an abundance of programming on cable which has finally made this medium attractive to people in urban areas. Just a decade ago, cable was used primarily in rural areas to bring in a clear signal that the terrain would block if sent through the air. Today, it's a national medium with specialized programming that broadcasting stations cannot normally offer—sporting events, movies and religious, children's or minority groups' coverage that traditional television has not the time for, access to, or interest in airing.

Combine this phenomenon with the fact that people are now willing to pay to receive more television programming, and you've got a field that is just wide open with potential. Last year, according to *Television Digest,* revenues from the cable industry were estimated at nearly $2 billion, whereas in the next five years, the revenues are anticipated to more than triple! *Just think what that means in terms of career growth potential.*

"The cable industry presents enormous opportunity for personal growth for young people with professional marketing, sales, and business skills," says Dave Shepard, President of David Shepard Associates, Inc., a major New York consulting firm to the cable and publishing industries.

"The industry is expanding at such a rapid rate," says Dave Shepard, "that despite its recent growth it is still staffed primarily by technical people—managers and executives who grew up with the business and whose basic skills and inclinations lie on the technical and engineering side of the business. With the advent of new programming opportunities, the cable industry is creating a huge demand for executives who have the knowledge and skills necessary to develop and market these new programming alternatives to a willing and waiting public. The opportunity is particularly bright for young people just out of business school."

Although cable programming is shown on the television set, don't go into the cable industry with the expectation of breaking into the commercial broadcasting stations. The reason is simple. Broadcasters (who send programming through the air) are prohibited by the Federal Communications Commission (FCC) to own cable systems (who send programming through a wire) for antimonopoly purposes. In other words, cable is the big, new form of competition to traditional television (commercial, mass-market broadcasting).

CABLE TELEVISION'S COMPETITOR, HOME VIDEO

Another major competitor (to commercial television broadcasting *and* cable) is the video market. This is defined as nonbroadcast television utilizing a video cassette or a video disc. Basically, there are two types of systems, those which allow you to record directly from a television set and to play back for future use, or those which play prerecorded material. It is the latter which poses the most serious "threat" to the commercial stations. Fortunately for them, the FCC does not restrict broadcasters from owning in the video market. As a result, all major networks are involved in this high growth market segment.

What makes this whole area of pay-for-programming growth so exciting is that at this moment, media executives still don't know which will take the lead, cable or video, or whether there will be a place for both.

Dave Shepard continues, "The big question regarding video over the next ten years has nothing to do with the technology. The question is just how much the average consumer will spend on a continuing basis for home entertainment. Cable companies are investing millions of dollars in new urban franchises and in rebuilding older suburban and rural franchises on the assumption that the average subscriber will not only take the basic cable service but also subscribe to two or three optional pay services. In current dollars, this means a monthly expenditure of $20-$30 for cable entertainment.

"At the same time, the suppliers of video discs are expecting equal numbers of consumers to spend equal sums of dollars on prepackaged video discs. If both the cable and the video people are correct, the average TV viewer will be spending $50-$60 per month on television entertainment. In addition, the video-cassette suppliers are equally optimistic and look to cable and its multiple sources of programming to spur the growth of its technology. Just which suppliers will survive this change in home entertainment viewing, and which will not survive, is a question that will eventually be answered—but only by the consumer."

BREAKING INTO BROADCASTING: A VIEW FROM THE INSIDE

A secretary and "back-up" production associate for a major television station in New York City had a terrific contact (her dad is an engineer for the station), who helped her get an internship with the station while she was still in college. She explains, "You can get in because of friends, but no further. You have to do that on your own."

For someone without contacts, she explains, "Well, it's very tight; they don't pick people off the streets." She leans forward, somewhat confidentially, "But they will hire for vacation relief —if you want to come in for six months and then be laid off. That's what I did." She continues, "But I came in here with the attitude that I had to get a job, so I worked my tail off. I was mainly on the assignment desk, which is right out there in the middle of the room where everyone could see me. And I really was very assertive; I wanted to make sure they knew who I was." She pauses, "Then I was just lucky. The guy who was on the reception desk got another job in the company and they asked me if I wanted the job. I said, 'Sure!' And I was willing to do anything and happy to do it. So along with receptionist I was made the back-up graphics coordinator—that's the person who makes sure the 'stills' (photographs or illustrations used in conjunction with a story) and the 'supers' (name captions and other superimposed text) are in the right places; it's a scheduling job. And I was working twelve hours a day, seven days a week, but," and she shrugs, "long hours come with the territory; you've just got to expect it. Anyway, then after that the regular production associate went on a vacation and I got to be 'back-up.'" Her eyes light up, "That's a control-room job, and timing is the big thing there. So during the broadcast I let them know, 'We're this much over, this much under.' I'd check the script and work with the director and the producer. Everyone liked me there. And you learn a hell of a lot! It's a *very* desirable job."

Looking ahead, she said, "At this point I want to get to be a full-time production associate, then associate director and then I'll take it from there. That's now. But I've changed my mind so many times. I have no delusions, though I never wanted to be on-camera. I tried it in school (she majored in Communications at Hofstra University), but I just wasn't comfortable on the air. So I thought I'd be a producer, but I'm not sure any more. There are so many jobs to do here. I've just got to put in my time. Me—I'm the type who wants everything tomorrow, but I've got to put in a year or two. And even if I don't necessarily want a particular job, I'll meet people."

Has she considered going out of town? "It's a decision. It's true you don't learn the field when you're in New York, but then who knows if I'd be guaranteed a job back here in ten years. New York is where I want to be; I was born and bred here and I don't want to leave. Anyway, you've got to be in New York or Los Angeles; if anything is going to happen in this business, it's going to happen in one of those two places. And who knows? I keep thinking as long as I'm in this building (her station is located in the same New York office building with the national NBC network), I could meet the President of the network in the elevator and impress the hell out of him." She laughs, "Thank God, it hasn't happened yet! I'd probably panic and go weak at the knees."

DOING YOUR HOMEWORK IN RADIO AND TELEVISION BROADCASTING, FILM FOR TELEVISION, CABLE TELEVISION, AND HOME VIDEO

As an introduction to this section, there is a good story that an executive at Twentieth Century-Fox Television tells about himself:

> I can still remember when I first went to work for this company, I had a lot of books at home about the film business, but I'd never read any of them. Anyway, I was in the office one Sunday afternoon and there was one other person in the office that day, so I introduced myself and he told me who he was. Well, the next day I happened to mention to my boss that I had met a man in the office yesterday and I asked who he was. My boss said, "He was on the Board of Directors with Darryl Zanuck." "Oh," I said, "Who's Darryl Zanuck?" He chuckled, "Well, Darryl Zanuck virtually *founded* this company." Believe me, after that I started reading.

ADVANCE READING

Broadcasting Yearbook (Broadcasting Publications, Inc.): Names and addresses of companies.

Film/Tape Production Source Book (Television/Radio Age; annual): All film/tape producers (production companies) in U.S. and Canada, with names of principals.

Getting into Film by Mel London (Ballantine Books, New York, 1977): More of the ins-and-outs of this business; includes chapter on the unions.

LOOK NOW, PAY LATER: The Rise of Network Broadcasting by Laurence Bergreen (Doubleday, 1980)

Television Production: Disciplines and Techniques by Thomas D. Burrows and Donald N. Wood (Wm. C. Brown, 1978): A very thorough introduction to television (tools, techniques, methods, materials, training exercises, creative purposes, studio procedures); one of the best, detailed books of what television is all about.

Your Future in Broadcasting by John R. Rider (Richard Rosen Press, 1978): A clear presentation of the field; production chapter includes job profiles.

How to Break into Motion Pictures, Television, Commercials and Modeling by Nina Blanchard (Doubleday, Garden City, 1978): Directed to actors and therefore relevant for anyone with ambitions for an on-camera career.

LEGENDS OF THE BUSINESS BY LEGENDS OF THE BUSINESS

As It Happened by William Paley (Doubleday, Garden City, 1979): A history of the conception and growth of CBS by its founder; well-written, easy-to-read; lots of stories about stars and major productions; a good view of the inside of an enormous communications empire.

Mike Douglas: My Own Story by Mike Douglas (Ballantine Books, New York, 1979): Anecdotes and situations from his life and career; a look at the "star" side of the business.

Cavett by Dick Cavett and Christopher Porterfield (Harcourt, Brace, Jovanovich, New York, 1974): Cavett is interviewed about his life and career; full of typically Cavett quips.

The Camera Never Blinks: Adventures of a TV Journalist by Dan Rather and Mickey Herskowitz (Ballantine Books, New York, 1977)

A Civil Tongue by Edwin Newman (Warner Books, New York, 1977)

Clearing the Air by Daniel Schorr (Berkeley Publishing, New York, 1978)

Cosell by Howard Cosell (Pocket Books, New York, 1974): The omnipresent sportscaster, without the voice.

Due to Circumstances Beyond Our Control by Alfred ("Fred") W. Friendly (Random House, New York, 1967)

Good Evening, Everybody by Lowell Thomas (Avon, New York, 1977)

Challenges of Change by Walter Cronkite (Public Affairs Press, Washington, D.C., 1971)

AFTER YOU GET THE JOB

The Broadcast Communications Dictionary, ed. by Lincoln Diamant (Hastings House, New York, 1978): This is it for the full range of terminology in the field.

The Best Thing on TV—Commercials by Jonathan Price (Penguin, New York, 1978): Any student of film, television, mass media, broadcasting or communications will benefit from the analysis of commercials in this book, of what went into them and what made them work.

Broadcast News Writing by G. Paul Smeyak (Grid Publishers, Inc., Columbus, Ohio, 1977): A how-to book; covers Style, Grammar, Lead-Ins, News Judgment, News Sources, Legal Judgments, etc.

KEY TRADE PUBLICATIONS

Television/Radio Age ($30 per year; Television Editorial Corp., 666 Fifth Avenue, New York, NY 10019)

Broadcasting ($50 per year; Broadcasting Publications, Inc., 1735 De Sales St., N.W., Washington, DC 20036)

Variety ($45 per year; Variety, Inc., 154 West 46th Street, New York, NY 10036)

Backstage ($32 per year; Backstage Publications, Inc., 165 West 46th Street, New York, NY 10036): Film production.

Billboard ($110 per year; Billboard Publications, Inc., One Astor Plaza, 1515 Broadway, New York, NY 10036): Record and radio industry.

About the Author

Caroline A. Zimmermann launched her career as a secretary in a New York magazine publishing firm. She moved from secretary to assistant and finally to a management position, then left publishing to join an advertising agency as an account executive. Shortly thereafter, Ms. Zimmermann moved on to found her own New York-based advertising agency, and over the years has achieved recognition as a marketing expert, reporter, author, lecturer, and photographer. She divides her time between New York City and Sag Harbor, Long Island.